John C. Hyland

"You Can't Handle The Truth!:

"UNMASKING 100 LIBERAL MYTHS, MEDIA BIAS,
and the
U.S. MORAL DECAY"!

"What Every American Should Read!"

john c. hyland

What are YOU going to do about it?

++++++++++++++++++++

God Promises a Safe Landing!!
Not a Safe Passage!!

++++++++++++++++++++

Order this book online at www.trafford.com/07-1944
or email orders@trafford.com

Most Trafford titles are also available at major online book retailers.

© Copyright 2008 John C. Hyland.

All rights reserved. No part of this publication may be reproduced, stored in a retrieval system, or transmitted, in any form or by any means, electronic, mechanical, photocopying, recording, or otherwise, without the written prior permission of the author.

Note for Librarians: A cataloguing record for this book is available from Library and Archives Canada at www.collectionscanada.ca/amicus/index-e.html

ISBN: 978-1-4251-4569-9

We at Trafford believe that it is the responsibility of us all, as both individuals and corporations, to make choices that are environmentally and socially sound. You, in turn, are supporting this responsible conduct each time you purchase a Trafford book, or make use of our publishing services. To find out how you are helping, please visit www.trafford.com/responsiblepublishing.html

Our mission is to efficiently provide the world's finest, most comprehensive book publishing service, enabling every author to experience success. To find out how to publish your book, your way, and have it available worldwide, visit us online at www.trafford.com/10510

www.trafford.com

North America & international
toll-free: 1 888 232 4444 (USA & Canada)
phone: 250 383 6864 ♦ fax: 250 383 6804
email: info@trafford.com

The United Kingdom & Europe
phone: +44 (0)1865 722 113 ♦ local rate: 0845 230 9601
facsimile: +44 (0)1865 722 868 ♦ email: info.uk@trafford.com

10 9 8 7 6 5 4 3

A Twelve Year Search and Investigation!

*DEDICATED TO MY COURAGEOUS
FRIENDS IN MY CONSERVATIVE GROUP*

*FOR ALL THEIR HELP, ENCOURAGEMENT
AND FAITH IN MY WORDS!!
MAY GOD BLESS AND
PROTECT THEM!!*

"And to my *fantastic* children, their
spouses and our grandchildren
for their
prayers and assistance"!!

"GOD BE WITH ALL OF YOU"!

john c. hyland

What are YOU going to do about it?

about the author

He really doesn't consider himself an author, but more of a statistical gatherer and political analyst. He has assembled data from many hundreds of sources and put it in one book. Most readers have heard or read most of these individual statistics and quotations over the years in the media, from the government, etc., but never has anyone put them all together, and added commentary, for the full scope of what is transpiring in the U. S. and how the Congressional liberal left, aided by the media, unions, ACLU, AARP, NEA, etc., is destroying our security, morality and strong family values.

Mr. Hyland, former Chamber of Commerce executive, former President of the Wisconsin Chamber of Commerce Executives, an Economic Developer, a business executive, a teacher, golf champion, U.S. Veteran, coach/athletic director, entrepreneur, businessman. Well known as a church fund-raiser and 80, still serves as a volunteer in many capacities in Church and School activities and has served several parishes as a lector and a Eucharistic Minister. A former school board member, Charter Grand Knight and District Deputy in the Knights of Columbus, officer in Rotary, member of Lions, Toastmasters and named to Commissions by the Governor and Congressman both in Tourism and Business. He has been to the Virgin Islands, Puerto Rico, Japan, Mexico, Ireland, Hawaii and Canada for additional experiences as well as most every State.

He has put on all day seminars for Chambers, Visitor Bureaus, Cities and Universities in the Midwest as a consultant on public

---

A Twelve Year Search and Investigation!

relations, tourism, business and promotions. He represented Wisconsin and the Great Lakes States on a trade mission to Japan. Now retired, Mr. Hyland has pursued a life of moral activism for the past 15 or more years. Encouraging ethical morals and traditional family values.

The following analysis and statistics came together in a 12-year information hunt. He has tried to authenticate all facts, and searched both sides of an issue as best as humanly possible. If anyone has *irrefutable* proof, any item in this book is inaccurate, please contact him for an immediate correction (possible with new technology) by contacting the publisher.

Please study every topic carefully. You'll find most items very revealing and *unreported or under-reported* by the nations estimated 80% liberal media and basically not known by much of the vulnerable, consistently liberally brainwashed, general public! Hours and hours every day have gone into watching most all networks including C-Spans, CNN, MSNBC, FOX, and regular news programs on national and local TV.

Many hours daily were also spent reading government, health agency, Congressional reports, etc. These and *indisputable experts* reporting on C-Span or in the news, were the main sources (usually two) for most of the material contained within! Some statistics may be a little off here or there (or even incorrect is possible considering the hundreds of stats involved) and because of the year they were collected, but that will not drastically change the over-all meaning of the message. He is known for honesty, integrity and an idea-man!

What are YOU going to do about it?

INDEX

Chapter I
	Page
Are We Ungrateful	9
Presidents Intelligence	15
Who Voted for Who	21
Liberals Just Don't Get It	27
Polls, Polls, Polls	35

Chapter II
Health and Social Costs	41
Cuts in Medicaid	47
Prescription Drugs	49
Cuts in Education	55
No Child Left Behind	61
Social Security	63

Chapter III
Global Warming	65
Hurricane Katrina	73
Population Explosion	75
Heating Homes	77
Price Gouging	79
Gas Prices	81
Oil Company Profit	85

A Twelve Year Search and Investigation!

Chapter IV
World Opinion.................................89
Coalitions....................................93
Intelligence Gathering........................95

Chapter V
Guard Deployment..............................99
Iraq and WMD'S...............................101
Casualties in Iraq...........................109
Atrocities...................................113
The War on Terror............................115
Defense Spending.............................123

Chapter VI
U.S. Moral Breakdown.........................127
Archaic U. S. Senate.........................133
Friends of the Helpless......................139
Illegal Immigration..........................141

Chapter VII
Economy and Jobs.............................149

Chapter VIII
Media Bias...................................167
Guilty Before Indictment.....................171

What are YOU going to do about it?

ARE YOU A CATHOLIC, CHRISTIAN and/OR A BELIEVER IN CHRISTMAS AND SUPPORT NATIVITY SCENES ??

As you know many cities, towns, states, and federal agencies have declared war on Nativity Scenes at Christmas time. More and more are forbidding these traditional Christmas displays in public places!

Would you be willing to help solve this problem?

What if every citizen at their homes and every store owner or business firm who agrees with this premise, would put up a Nativity scene on their own property?

Would that not be great? Let's show these radical atheists and liberal judges that we can do it on our own and don't need the government's help.

So, how about it? Start shopping around for a scene that would go in front of your house or business or on the roof or on the porch roof, etc.

We can do it...... Start planning now!!

john c. hyland

A Twelve Year Search and Investigation!

CHAPTER I

ARE WE UNGRATEFUL?

Worthy of note, is the latest (mid-summer 2007) poll numbers, showing that the liberal media and the democrats have brainwashed much of the gullible public into believing and agreeing with the bias hammered into them on a daily basis on what they think about America and if they are happy or not with the way the Country is going.

A huge 67% of people are unhappy. What are they unhappy about? An unknown author and I give our combined and unique explanation! **What do you think?**

"*Are they unhappy* with the complete religious, social and political freedoms we enjoy that are the envy of the world or are they unhappy because they have electricity and running water 24 hours a day or maybe because they have air conditioning in the summer and heat in the winter? Everyone who wants a job and can handle one and/or qualify, has a job.

"*Or how about* the ability to walk or easily get to the numerous super markets that provide us with the greatest array of fresh fruits, vegetables, etc., available anywhere or maybe it's the freedom to drive from New York to California without having to show identification to police or military even though passing through many states?

"*Or perhaps* having clean and safe motels and nice restaurants when traveling? How about the great array of car service facilities if your car breaks down? They'll even send a helicopter to fetch you if injured on our highways!

"*Maybe* you're one of the 70% who own their own homes but don't like the idea that well-trained and well-equipped firemen will come immediately if you have a fire or maybe the police who come bravely to help if you have a break-in or are attacked!

"*Are you unhappy* because most neighborhoods are free from the threat of bombs or military raping or pillaging the residents?

A Twelve Year Search and Investigation!

"Seems like we might be an ungrateful bunch of spoiled brats! We happen to be the most blessed in the world and we should be thanking the good Lord we live here. More college graduates than ever with near 30% with degrees compared to 8% a few decades ago. More owning their own homes than ever. 1 out of 3 African Americans are now in the middle class compared to just 1 out of 10 a couple of decades ago.

"*And get this:* 58% of those with incomes of $30,000 or less, feel their federal income taxes are **too high**.....and did you know....*THEY DON'T PAY ANY* ! In fact, government programs give them back in services, food stamps, etc., as much as they make in income. *They spend twice what they earn.* THIS proves that the public has been brainwashed by the Democrats into believing that the rich get all the tax breaks...*EVEN THOUGH*...now get this...*the top 50% of income earners pay 96% of all* taxes. The bottom 50% pay only 4%! *WHO'S* getting the breaks?

"*Oh! I know!* You are unhappy with the President. **Is that it?** The same President who guided the nation after the dark days of 9-11! The same President who cut our taxes to bring the economy out of recession and given us the best economy ever! Is this the same

---

What are YOU going to do about it?

President who has been called every name in the book and bashed by the liberal media and Democrats for succeeding to keep all Americans safe from further terrorist attacks!

"Has the President caused you personal pain, or is it just because *the media told you he was failing*? He is the commander-in-chief of the military that is defending all your freedoms and they didn't have to go, they are *all volunteers*. There is currently no draft in the U.S. I blame the media and the liberals who slam the President at every turn and refuse to say anything positive about the greatest economy in the world and the greatest freedoms in the world! They just refuse to *TELL IT LIKE IT IS.....* because they want to win the next election...........regardless the consequences! BASH, BASH, BASH!!!

"It may be time to turn off your national news on our nearly all-liberal TV stations and quit reading our newspapers. Burn "Newsweek' and "Time" and use the New York Times for the bottom of your bird cage. Then start feeling grateful for all we have in this country and thank God every day. At least be thankful and appreciative! I really don't think it's right to take God out of the Pledge of Allegiance, money, or from public buildings or schools as a few radical, liberal atheists and secular judges want to do!"

Have you ever wondered what happened to the 56 signers of the Declaration of Independence? They signed and *they pledged their lives,* their fortunes and their sacred honor. **What kind of men were they?**

Twenty-four were lawyers and jurists, eleven were merchants and nine were farmers and large plantation owners. All were men of means, well educated. But they signed the Declaration of Independence knowing full well that *the penalty would be death* if they were captured by the British.

Five signers were captured by the British as traitors and tortured before they died. Twelve had their homes ransacked and burned. Two lost their sons serving in the army and another had two sons captured. Nine of the 56 fought *and died* from their wounds or hardships of the war.

Some of us take these liberties too much for granted. So, on the next 4'th of July, take a few minutes to silently or publicly thank these patriots.
AND GOD BLESS AMERICA !!!!!

What are YOU going to do about it?

FOR IMMEDIATE RELEASE:

Organizations, clubs, groups of any kind are reminded that Mr. Hyland is available to appear at your meetings or functions at no cost except expenses and to be given an opportunity to make his book available to those in attendance. He does have the privilege of refusing any group because of time constraints and his health. Please contact the Publisher who will make the contact for you. Thanks and God Bless!

john c. hyland

AUTHOR AND CONSULTANT

A Twelve Year Search and Investigation!

PRESIDENT'S INTELLIGENCE!

*T*he President graduated from Yale and has a Masters degree. *(Not easy)!* He was also trained to pilot a very complicated F-102 fighter jet in the National Guard. *(Not easy)!* His instructor said **he was one of the top 5% he every trained**. Also, new records, released recently, **PROVED** that the President did in fact, complete all his National Guard requirements (**contrary to** loud previous liberal accusations and insinuations).

The President was also a successful businessman and at one time owned a major league baseball team. (Not easy)! Most Senators and Congressmen never had or even tried to be successful in business, economics, or any kind of people management positions etc. Politicians/attorneys to the core, from the start!

Gore flunked out of Vanderbilt grad school (5 F's) and withdrew early another time, yet, was considered the brain by our "intelligent" media. (His only creditable choice...politics). His high school records were nearly as bad. Kerry's college grades were basically the same as the Presidents and even a bit lower. Give credit for

---

What are YOU going to do about it?

his short military service where he was given three controversial Purple Hearts (called band-aid wounds by men he served with and doctors who treated him). Both made to be politicians from the get-go!!

Clinton, *the true draft dodger*, ran against two war heroes in 1992 and 1996 for the Presidency and **military service never became an issue** in the media, but yet, Bush was *crucified by the media* and liberal democrats for his National Guard efforts in the last election. **Remember that?** Once again, double standard in full view! *No question!!*

Recently, new information about the Clinton draft dodging has surfaced. It is now reported that Clinton was ordered to report for induction after being drafted in 1969 *(he failed to report).* He then was reclassified 1-D after quickly enlisting in the Arkansas University ROTC, *to escape the draft,* through the efforts of Col. Eugene Holmes of the University's ROTC, (who later said that he was mislead by Clinton in a two hour interview, not divulging that he, Clinton, *had organized and led anti-American and anti-war* demonstrations in England while in college there).

But then, Clinton *again failed to report* to the University for ROTC (after writing and thanking Colonel Holmes for saving him from the draft) *and never served* after that because of a glitch in the draft numbering system. He was able *to play the system and made it work!* (Pretty much normal for him)! Not much in the U.S. media! MORE DOUBLE STANDARDS !

Yet liberals, democratic talking heads, Hollywood celebrities and radical TV comedians continually make fun and humiliate President Bush with endless jokes and ridicule on a **nightly basis** on the Tonight Show and the Late Show with Leno and Letterman besides a few other lesser comedy shows and some morning talk shows. The most dangerous TV personality, MSNBC's Keith Olberman, *crucifies the President nearly every night,* not just ridiculed by jokes, but inflammatory, humiliating, commentary opinion. Of course, the anti-Christian Maher and Stewart are not far behind. Again, liberals **brainwashing the public** at every TURN!

The office of the President has suffered great harm in the last seven years because of the inflammatory remarks by the liberals. It has been further eroded by the entertainment industry with their bashing, anti-

---

What are YOU going to do about it?

American movies and TV and unfounded claims against the President. *How really sad!!*

And maybe even worse is the fact that much of this "reporting" and bashing **is picked up by the European and Arab networks** for broadcast *world wide.*

It is very obvious every night on TV, with young Letterman and Leno audiences, laughing and agreeing, that much **of the young public is completely BRAINWASHED.** But, it seems that President Bush's *only real problem* is miss-pronouncing a few words. How terrible!! **Crucify him!!!** Have you ever mispronounced a word or two? *We all have!* Frequently!

Did the Democrats and the media give you the impression that Gore had really won the 2000 election and it was stolen by the Republicans? Consider that Bush won 29 states, Gore 19. Population of counties that Bush won, 143 million, Gore 127 million. Murder rate in Bush counties, 2.1 per 100,000, Gore counties 13.2. Bush territory predominately taxpayer owned. Gore's, a lot of government owned tenements and those living off various forms of government welfare. Draw your own conclusions!!!

A Twelve Year Search and Investigation!

Going a little further on this topic: there are near 200 million registered voters. 50 million voted for Gore! Does that sound like a majority as the liberal democrats like to shout from the housetops? Which means that 150 million did not vote for Gore (although they could have--WHY NOT)? Also, Bush won 2,436 counties and Gore 677. Bush, square miles, 2.5 million---Gore, 600,000.

Then in fact, DESPITE being the incumbent, DESPITE the good economy, DESPITE MANY women supporting abortions, DESPITE the near total support of minorities, DESPITE the support of the nations liberal media, DESPITE the backing of the liberal Hollywood crowd, DESPITE the support of most women's organizations, DESPITE the HORRENDOUS scare tactics used on Seniors, DESPITE the heavily Democratic Florida Courts ---- Gore could only come close!! Why?? One thing is sure, the voters remembered the sleeze of the DRAFT DODGING Clinton administration! Could that be it? Or maybe Gore's 5 F's. Whatever!

Clinton also had a Democrat Senate and House when entering office and left with a Republican Senate and House eight years later! *Why??* Hmm....

What are YOU going to do about it?

A SERIOUS <u>PERPETUATED</u> LIBERAL MYTH……..

When President Bush landed on the deck of the a naval carrier returning to port after several months on duty, there was a sign that said :

"MISSION ACCOMPLISHED"

Unfortunately, this quote was attributed to the President…..

The sign was actually put up by the Commander of the Carrier and he was just giving credit to his personnel for a tour well done!!

It did NOT refer to Iraq….
as the media, liberals and politicians said at the time and keep repeating to this day…….nearly every day!!!!!!!!
Even though it has been explained to them!!!

ANYTHING TO DISCREDIT THE PRESIDENT !!

WHO VOTED FOR WHO?

*D*id you know that the majority of Christians supported the President and voted for him in the 2004 election? Especially **those who attend Church** regularly! Also, the **more a person is educated**, the more he voted for Bush. Highly trained and educated managers, supervisors, CEO's, CFO's, corporate owners, etc., mostly voted for Bush. The few educated groups not voting for Bush were the extreme, radical ACLU and the highly liberal education union members and professors.

Areas in the nation going for Kerry were mostly the East and West Coast liberal bastions, the big cities and other areas with large union blue collar and minority factions and smaller cities that have a big population of college students, union blue collar workers and University faculty like Madison and La Crosse in Wisconsin.

Interestingly, the metropolitan Fox Valley/Green Bay area in Wisconsin went for Bush (1/2 million population). (Highly educated area and a mostly nonunion, excellent work force). One of the few metro areas in the country that went for the President!

Have you ever noticed that the Democrats **always** court the blue collar union workers, gays, African-Americans, the 18 to 25 year old group (50% of college *students cannot understand an editorial*, some can't even tell you **who's buried in Grants Tomb—proven on TV**). Then there are ex-cons, young vulnerable females because of the abortion issue, the poor, our senior citizens and immigrants. Does that tell you something?

YES! Most of these are the most vulnerable and easiest to influence and are the least educated! It is very obvious from listening and reading public opinions that over 50% of the general public have really no interest in, and no incentive, to read or learn about the problems our government is involved in or who is running for office (the numbers reflect the voting percentages).

Recently, **supporters** of the newly elected Democrat Congressman from Wisconsin's Fox Valley, Steve Kagen, publicly said that they voted for Kagen because they wouldn't vote for a Republican. How intelligent is that? They since have found out and now realize, they have elected an arrogant joke for Congress. Is that great or what? Only a few union bosses have been offering any support with ridiculous TV commercials *(paid by unions)* saying how great he is and how he was responsible for having the minimum wage passed in Congress. (**If it wasn't for a Democratic shakedown and attaching the wage bill to another needed bill at the last minute, (that the minority wanted), in the Senate and the Republicans allowing it to go through, there would not have been a minimum wage passed).** *It could have been blocked* easily by the Republicans, *if they desired,* (they were not against it). His whole campaign was typical liberal. Just **tell the people what they want to hear,** depending on the audience.

Can you believe, I sent the Congressman a pre-published, smaller version of this book during his campaign in 2006. He called me the next day and said he agreed with most everything in the book and wanted to sit down and visit with me. He would have his secretary call me for an appointment. It never happened. We never talked. Hummmmm!.

What are YOU going to do about it?

I think it rather interesting that most of the big pushes to register voters are in the **minority areas** of big cities and campuses organized by liberals. Easiest to manipulate because they have no idea what or who they are voting for. These are widely promoted and publicized by the media. Same with young eligible voters. Big pushes by liberals on campuses to get them registered although *most haven't a clue on the issues* or the candidates and that is why they typically do not vote--**plus a lot of apathy !**

The Democrats, every election, base their political agenda on taking care of the poor, the needy, give health benefits to all, let ex-cons vote, permit gays to marry and of course their main goal is take from the rich and *give to the poor which is called communism*!! (Somebody please tell them that, in 2005, **the richest 50 % paid nearly 96% of all taxes** and the bottom 50% paid 4%)! Of course, they want **more**... *and* **more**... *and* **more**!!!

The Democrats *always promise the world* to the poor but *seldom deliver.* Taxes would have **to double** to pay for their proposed programs -- **that never come through!** Best example of that are education, immigration and health care that they completely failed on during the 8 Clinton years and so far in 2007! If everyone was on welfare, fine with liberals.

The general public didn't want any part of the Hillary proposed national health care program similar to those in many other countries (**that are failing miserably and hated by their citizens**). Canada and Ireland are great examples. I've been there and talked to these people. (In fact Canada is now talking about privatizing health care and **doing away with socialized** health that does not work).

A 2007 movie documentary by the "loveable", radical, **psychotic** Michael Moore, bashed our nations health care system (although **best in the world**), tried to give some health care statistics that mostly were proven wrong and generally tried to scare the public into getting rid of the current administration by once again spewing many pure lies like his other, previous attack documentary, aimed at the Bush Administration. His movies failed miserable!

It was reported that even the Canadian Parliament and the Press **have known to bash the health system** in Canada. Mr. Moore feels that doctors and hospitals, should not make a profit. To show his lack of understanding and that his evidence gathering is really horrific, *85% of hospital beds* in the U.S. are already *nonprofit hospitals* and one that Moore bashed, Kaiser Permanente, is also nonprofit. In fact the *Supreme Court in Canada* declared that the government health care monopoly *is a violation of human rights.*

How *they treat Seniors* could be a whole new book and a *real serious matter* ! Over 3 million Canadians are *waiting to get a primary doctor.* (Out of 32 million). Canada is also way down when comparing the other 28 major industrialized nations *as they rank* 24th for the number of doctors per thousand.

INNOCENCE IS PRICELESS

One Sunday morning, the pastor noticed little Alex standing in the foyer of the Church staring at a plaque. It was covered with names with small American flags mounted on either side of it.

The seven year old had been staring at the plaque for some time, so the pastor walked up, stood behind the little boy, and said quietly, "Good morning Alex."

"Good morning Pastor," he replied, still focused on the plaque. Pastor, "what is this?" he asked.

The Pastor said, "Well son, it's a memorial to all the young men and women who died in the service."

Soberly, they just stood together staring at the large plaque.

Finally, little Alex's voice, barely audible and trembling with fear, asked, "Which service, the 8:30 or the 10:45?"

LIBERALS JUST DON'T GET IT !!!

*T*hey lost the 2004 election because of OVER-THE-TOP BASHING AND MIS-REPRESENTATION of the President by the media, radical, ultra-bashing organizations like the *billionaire funded* Move-on.org and liberals the likes of Kennedy, Clinton, Pelosi, Michael Moore, Al Franken, Howard Dean, Durbin, Reid, Boxer, Kerry, Feingold, Leahy, Dorgin, Olberman, Specter, vanden Heuvel, et-al! And they are all still staying the same course! What a break for the Republicans. It nearly guarantees a Conservative Presidential victory in 2008! Those liberals mentioned above are probably the most *dangerous people in America.*

I frequently hear the question:
"What is a Liberal"?
We frequently hear and I find it strange, but easy to see why, many *Democrats hate to admit* and they refuse to be called, "liberals". All one has to do is look at the far reaching base of the party and you'll find a multitude of wacky, radical, "out-of-the-mainstream" political and social groups **who call themselves Liberal**

What are YOU going to do about it?

Democrats and support Democrat candidates but yet *no one* wants to be associated with these groups.

We're talking about the Democrat liberals, who they themselves, **support or encourage groups** who support, gay marriage, abortion on demand, the ACLU and atheists keeping the words and displays of Christmas and God out of government and schools and removing mention of God from money and government buildings, requiring senior centers to eliminate prayer, removing crosses from Veteran Cemeteries and War Memorials or firing a worker in a library for wearing a pendant shaped like a cross.

PLUS, legalization of marijuana, the new abortion pill without a prescription and other drugs. They also accept the views of many *radical atheists* who continually force very radical minority views through legal means. In addition there are those who support euthanasia, embryonic stem cell research, cloning and many groups supporting anti-Christian/Catholic bashing and Universities de-funding conservative Christian groups because they require "Christian leadership" or just because they are conservative.

A Twelve Year Search and Investigation!

Then there are those liberals like secular professors, secular judges and the uniformed, secular Hollywood, over-the-top elite, who continue to put out immoral trash, violence, sex, foul language and political propaganda on the big screen, on TV, in the classroom and from the bench. Films and TV shows are getting *more and more anti-administration, anti-American*, highly secular and vulgar to the core. Much of the **propaganda** is very subtle. Many films these days, by the big stars, are completely liberal biased and highly immoral. Then there are a few un-elected judges forcing States to recognize same sex marriage. Have you noticed that the popular "Law & Order" TV series are nearly all anti-administration, anti-government and anti-Christian. Subtle but there!

Movie examples: In 2006, out of the 6 most honored movies, four had suggestive themes. One of the most acclaimed was "Brokeback Mountain". This movie had *continuous and excessive* smoking, drinking, explicit gay sex, explicit sex, divorces, nudity, numerous beatings, excessive anger, crude language. Two others that were acclaimed included anti-American or anti-Israel themes, "Syrania" and "Munich".

What are YOU going to do about it?

"Departed", (a Director Scorses movie starring DiCaprio, Nicholson, Damon, Martin Sheen, and Alex Baldwin -- *all six radical liberal leftists*), had 2½ hours of super violence, foul language and attacked Catholics, Priests, Ethnics, the Knights of Columbus, Police and the City of Boston. PLUS, they used the "F" word *near 200 times* and close to a 100 violent, graphic, on screen killings, with lots of blood and many beatings, crushing heads, etc. And can you believe the *Associated Press* reviewed the movie in typical liberal fashion, said, "*this is want we want in a Scorses film*"!

Have you noticed that Leno and Letterman (and others on TV) are getting **more and more graphic** with sexual innuendoes, body language and encouraging these types of movies with star interviews? All loved and viewed by young audiences! Do we have a moral problem??? You bet!!! *And it's growing fast!!*

Then in 2005 we had the highly rated movie "Closer", which had very graphic sexuality, nudity, disturbing images, drug use and extremely crude humor and was honored and acclaimed. My wife and I attended (because it was acclaimed) and watched as *about half the audience walked out* after the first 30 minutes. (Have you ever witnessed that before...I never had)?

GET THIS---The best "foreign film" of 2006 was a Palestinian movie *glorifying suicide bombers* who attack Israel and Iraq. Are we all OK with this? Seems so. Do we have a moral breakdown??? *Is there any question??*

There are also the ultra liberal union bosses in the National Education Association who have brainwashed teachers and continue to prevent us from having school systems in many areas that really teach and have forced us into paying enormous per student costs but we have received little back to support these tax busting school systems throughout the country (see info on education). Certainly, there are many exceptions to this around the country.

Of course we cannot forget the *extremely racist* NAACP leadership who usually *FAIL TO speak* for the majority of African Americans and bash and ridicule the President and the Republicans on most every major issues.

How can any moral person support any of the above? Even with all the media and liberal shenanigans, the

Presidents ratings have been between 30% and 40% or a little over or under, but *did you know the Democrat leader ratings in 2006 had slipped to 23%!* (Never mentioned by the media). And then the ratings for Congress dropped further in 2007, *down to 14%* after the liberals took over in January. (And oh, by the way, the *media had a 28% rating*, down from 37% a few years ago). Hmmm! I guess much of the public does realize that bashing, attacking, obstructionism, is not in their best interests in creating a better, more moral and thriving U.S. **MANY** Americans **CAN SEE THRU THIS!** Thank God!

During 2003 to 2006, liberal Democratic leaders in Congress continually threatened a filibuster to force 60 votes to make sure the Republicans could not pass any meaningful legislation (the conservative leaders are using the same tactic 2007) and the leaders of NEA, ACLU, NAACP, AARP, NOW and 80% of national press and TV *distorted and mislead the public* by giving a liberal spin on most all national issues, (many of which are discussed within).

You seldom see a happy or smiling Democrat leader. They are usually angry, ranting and raving. Always obstructing and bashing the *President every time* they *open their mouths!!* Completely political just to win an election!!

They seldom, if ever, support anything that is an idea or resolution brought by Republicans. Always tearing down and personalizing any initiative or insisting on dozens of changes that frequently killed the initiative. No matter what it was! Minority leader in the House, Nancy Pelosi, came right out and announced in 2005 that the Democrats would not agree to anything proposed by the Republicans or the President!! IS THIS THE WAY TO RUN A GOVERNMENT BY THE PEOPLE??

Why the extreme hate by liberal democrats and the nations media for the *President of the United States*? (*Even before the problems in Iraq*). Most think it is just to win an election! It is mind-boggling! There is also considerable proof and it has been reported, that many liberals, *35%, hoped for a bad economy* and a *defeat in Iraq.* How sick is that? A very recent poll *proved* these figures.

An interesting observation came upon my desk the other day. Evidently it had been circulated on the Internet and arrived in my e-mail. It goes like this:

"It sure isn't easy to differentiate democrats from terrorists these days!

Both Democrats and terrorists want American troops out of Iraq!
Both Democrats and terrorists hate George W. Bush!
Both Democrats and terrorists claim that American troops are killing and harassing innocent women and children!
Both Democrats and terrorists claim that American troops are an occupying force!
Both Democrats and terrorists claim that the war in Iraq was all about oil!
Both Democrats and terrorists claim that Bush LIED to get the Congress to agree to the war against Saddam.
Both Democrats and terrorists claim that America is losing the war in Iraq!
Both Democrats and terrorists claim that Bush RUSHED into the war!
   (Although **it took a year of delay** while gathering numerous U.N. and Congressional authorizations)!

But, to be sure, there is **ONE WAY** to tell democrats from terrorists: the Democrats **CLAIM** that they support the troops, while terrorists don't!!"

A Twelve Year Search and Investigation!

POLLS, POLLS, POLLS!!!

*P*olls of the Presidents good or bad rating are *completely media and liberal democrat driven.* All the public hears daily are the negative bashing thrown out by the nations liberal media and politicians. *What are they to believe?* Completely brainwashed!

You can watch C-Span mornings and evenings and watch Democratic Senators and Congressmen in their Chambers, *strictly talking to the camera* and the C-Span audience *with no one else in the Chamber*--obviously putting on the liberal spin---for hours at a time. Frequently you'll see forums of so-called *professor experts* on a stage, in an auditorium, giving their views (most all liberals), with hardly anyone in the auditorium, that holds hundreds---*strictly talking* to the sponsoring C-Span camera and audience.

And now a new problem has arisen. One liberal news network has been broadcasting Muslim or Arab speakers (usually a few liberal professors with far east type names or heads of Muslim organizations) supporting terrorists and condemning the U.S. and

---

What are YOU going to do about it?

Israel for protecting themselves and taking the fight to the terrorists.

One also repeats TV broadcasts from the Arab networks and *only shows the carnage and bombings every newscast* with *very negative reporting* from an *on-site extremely liberal reporter*. Daily you can see in most liberal newspapers like the New York Times, that negative stories are page one, while anything good that may have happened or reported, goes on page 10 on the bottom or not reported at all. This manipulation can be *seen daily in most every paper and on TV.* Examine the headline, then look at the story. Very revealing! Frequently, the positive side of the story will be in the last two paragraphs after a negative story line for most of the story.

Polls are *very easy to manipulate.* How the question is framed, what is asked, who is asked (are they liberals or conservatives, are they young or old, big city or small town America, voters or non-voters, education level, employed or not, etc.)? There has been several good books on the subject and many recent polls have been proven to be liberal biased. Unfortunately the public sees the poll results almost daily and is *brainwashed* into believing they are accurate.

When most every major newspaper and magazine, most every major TV network, *is liberally biased*, its easy to see how the polls, *they conduct*, reflect the liberal view. (And don't believe they aren't liberal---many excellent books have been written that have *proven all this*).

You'll frequently hear on the liberal networks or by liberal spokesmen or liberal newspapers, that Fox News is biased the other way. Do not believe this! They are one of the few news sources that will provide *both sides of every issue*. They usually have guest speakers or analysts that consists of both conservatives and liberals.

You seldom see this on any other network. (In fact, most of the time others will have several liberals or just one, giving their biased opinion on the same show--MSNBC and all of NBC, has the most liberal broadcasters although CNN, PBS and CBS are close).

Interestingly, MSNBC has dropped many live shows, late evenings, early morning and weekends. They have cut employees severely because of ratings and as of July 2007 they no longer are much of a factor in the news business.

Many would also find it interesting, that all of the newspapers called, "Army Times – "Navy Times" – "Air Force Times", etc., are all Gannett owned liberal papers *with reporters and editorial writers all liberals.* They are not official military papers. (Same company that puts out THE LIBERAL U.S.A. Today). Is this common knowledge?

Most always the major networks and newspaper editorials *give the liberal slant and spin only!* And remember, all reach international audiences and are widely reported *worldwide*! Everything negative is quickly picked up by Arab media! The liberals hate FOX *because they give both sides of an issue* and not just the liberal view!

There must be a reason why FOX has been the top cable news network for over six years and frequently *has more viewers* than MSNBC, CNBC, CNN and PBS *combined!* FOX has the three top prime time programs on cable, plus the top morning show and the top financial shows on cable. Some figures in 2007, showed that on FOX, "The Factor", on cable, had grown to around 4 million nighttime viewers while CBS evening news with the liberal Katy Couric had slipped to around 6 million. Getting close! Unheard of! It has been reported recently that FOX had the top 22 shows on cable. Most of the public realizes what's going on!! We all can't be fooled all the time! Unfortunately, *many of the most vulnerable* public believes what the national media tells them!

So, when you hear a liberal say they have every right to say it, (**even if damaging to our national security**)----that is true---but---*and this is a big but*--when the whole international community hears it, including the Arab nations, **it gives the enemy** the fortitude to continue killing U.S. soldiers, their coalition partners and innocent civilians. Is it really worth it? Or do they just hate the President so much they don't care! *TREASON??* You be the judge!

In 2006 when the British and U.S. authorities reported the *huge terror plot of blowing up 10 U.S. airliners* over the Atlantic and arresting 24 terrorists, audience call-ins on C-Span that same morning, about 4 out of 10 said, "*they did not believe a word of it as the President is a liar and we can't believe anything he says*". But yet the Democratic liberal leaders and the media *don't get it* and *think it doesn't hurt* our country to ridicule the President and say they have every right to say these things? WOW ! How patriotic!

What are YOU going to do about it?

It really shows how many have been *brainwashed!! Nearly 40%!*

In a similar vein, a 2007 poll showed *that nearly 1/3* of those polled, believed that the President planned the 9-11 attack on the World Trade Center by using arson and explosives from the ground up. (More *proof of brainwashing*)! These types of comments sure wouldn't have happened in WWII. "Zip it up" was the theme of the day and *do not help our enemies. Some have even claimed* that no planes hit the towers on 9-11 even though engines were recovered at the scene, videos of the planes, the crashes and the massive jet fuel explosions plus millions of TV eyewitnesses have proven it beyond any question!

HITLER said, "The big lie will eventually be accepted as the truth"! All these radical ideas came from a few liberal, evidently psychotic, Bush bashing professors and then picked up by left wing, extremely radical, liberal internet bloggers who were able to make it a public issue! *Really sick!* (One of main professors was from the University of Wisconsin and another from Colorado. It is now evident that one cannot believe anything on the internet as well over 50% is totally fabrication. Which is which though???

CHAPTER II

HEALTH & SOCIAL COSTS:

*W*hy have health costs increased? Simple! Our life style and the refusal to adjust and eliminate four huge reasons (listed below), which for the most part are *preventable!*

Obviously there are other reasons like shortage of health providers AND THE INCREASED NUMBERS NEEDING SERVICES, but much is caused by:

1. *Smoking:* 400,000 die every year! 40% of smokers will die from their habit! Millions are medically treated for **dozens** of lung problems including cancer, plus nursing home costs, lost wages, etc., all from smoking......**billions** of dollars. Easily preventable!!! 3 out of 4 homes now ban smoking. Some states and dozens of cities have now banned smoking also and it may not be long and we will have a permanent solution. Pray!!! It will save us Billions, maybe Trillions and *add years to thousands of lives*!

What are YOU going to do about it?

2. *Obesity:* Many studies show that near 1/3 of all children are now obese and that figure is expected to rise to 1/2 in the next few years.....billions are and will be spent on this preventable problem. Plus, we're not even talking about the millions of adults (1 in every 3 are obese) in the same situation when one considers that nearly $50 BILLION is *spent annually* on diet fads and programs plus many undergo *unnecessary, very expensive* surgery. *All preventable!* Tragically 800 die daily, (*that's daily*), from obesity related problems! Obesity cost: $100 Billion annually.

3. *Alcoholism:* How about the billions spent on treatment plus the many social problems that this so-called "disease" brings, (a disease coming from a bottle, no virus, no medical reasons, and no different than smoking, drug or other addictions). The lost wages, the social costs of divorces, families broken and the tragedy of near *15,000 killed* each and every year by drunk drivers! *All preventable!* See additional stats in our chapter on Moral Breakdown!

4. *Illegal drugs:* The medical and social costs are enormous going well into the billions, perhaps trillions. $180 million is *spent daily* by your fellow neighbors **just purchasing illegal drugs**......not

including the costs of enforcement, prison and treatment. *$17 Billion* is spent annually in the U.S. by government agencies **fighting drugs**! ALL very *PREVENTABLE!!!*

And the list goes on and on! And many complain about the billions being spent in our fight against terrorists----but how many wasted billions, even *trillions* from the four problems above—FAR MORE *THAN ANY TEN WARS!*

But, of course, *blame it on the President!* Obviously, the person themselves, parents and all citizens *refusing to take their own responsibility* is certainly the #1 reason! Health education, law enforcement and liberal judges, who frequently give light sentences and try to be politically correct, can also help prevent much of the problem.

The liberals also *continually argue* that somewhere near 40 or more million are without health insurance. They continue to blame the President and the Republicans for the problem although the problem *has always been around.* But when we investigated we found that about 1/3 **are in the upper income bracket** and *could purchase any insurance* they wanted but *fail to do* so. Another 1/3 *are eligible for government* health programs *but fail to take advantage.* And 1/3 are a group that consist of millions of illegal aliens *who are not eligible.* (From the Insurance Industry).

Many thousands of Native Americans on tribal lands also do not have decent medical services or insurance. Are they included in any of these groups? One Reservation has a very lucrative casino operation. It's a small tribe of only several hundred members. Each member is given a share of the proceeds that amounts to thousands of dollars per person, per year. Each has a large home in well-established neighborhoods and live elegant lives. But, they rely on *governments for education and health.* They have no schools and no hospitals or clinics. Just lots of money and a lavish life style.

This *leaves far less than the 40+ million* that the liberals keep ranting about. It now appears that maybe *only 8 million* and not 40+ million. Many of the those 8 million are eligible for many private drug company and government programs and can take advantage of free clinics, etc., that are in most cities. Many of these without insurance are part of the 3% who are lost in the cracks, the homeless, drug addicts, *those no one can reach*. Again, somewhat serious, but not the problem that the liberals keep screaming about from the rooftops! *Misleading* to say the least!

Seldom do we hear the media talking about how the *millions of illegal immigrants* are nearly all without health insurance and are most all in low paying jobs which *brings the health and job statistics down* abnormally lower than they really are. For example: over 2/3 of all births in Los Angeles County (population of 10.2 million) are to illegal aliens on Medi-cal, a California tax funded health aid for the poor. (L.A.Times). The nations media and liberal politicians would rather harp on the higher statistics for political reasons.

Another new report shows that an estimated 25% of health costs in America are *the results of litigation.* Thousands of purely irrelevant and speculative law suits over various medical procedures and results are filed annually. So our dear attorneys are making a fortune going after doctors, hospitals, etc., and making fortunes as did John Edwards. How many Billions or even maybe Trillions are going that route. *Of course, blame the President!*

What are YOU going to do about it?

The Democrats took over Congress in 2006

Prior to that, consumer confidence stood at a 2 & ½ year high.
Regular Gasoline sold for $2.19 per gallon.
Unemployment rate was 4.5%.

Since Democrats took over:
  Consumer confidence plummeted,
  Regular Gasoline is up to over $3.60 per gallon,
    (Pelosi promised to fix the gas costs).
  Unemployment is up to 5.5% (20% increase),
  Americans have lost $2.3 trillion in stock losses,
  Home equity has dropped by $1.2 trillion,
  1% of American homes are in foreclosure.

Yup! We voted for a change….and we got it!!

THAT'S NOT ALL…….

TAXES UNDER:	Clinton	Bush
Single making 30K:	$8,400	$4,500
Single making 75K:	$23,250	$18,750
Married making 60K:	$16,800	$9,000
Married making 125K:	$38,750	$31,250

REMEMBER: Congress passes all laws, not the President!

A Twelve Year Search and Investigation!

CUTS IN MEDICAID:

*T*he liberals have been shouting this myth for years and in *reality Medicaid has doubled* from $89.1 Billion in 1995 to $181.7 Billion in 2005 under President Bush and the Republican Congress. As of 2006, 18 *million recipients had been added since 2000*. Same with Food stamps *that rose 49.6%.*

Spending on social programs *rose $1.3 trillion* in 2005, *up 22% in last 5 years*. But, if you listen to the liberal ranting it seems that the President wants to, or has been, cutting all these programs.

The five-year period also had enrollment increases in child nutrition programs, unemployment compensation, veterans benefits, etc. More brainwashing when the liberals keep harping to the public that the *President is cutting everything* and *reported regularly by the liberal media!*

What are YOU going to do about it?

Hillarys education of Pennsylvania's voters!

NOT JUST MYTHS BUT LIES !!

Donald Lambro, chief political correspondent of the Washington Times and nationally syndicated columnist had an interesting view of Hillary Clinton's many speeches during the Pennsylvania primaries. She said many times that, **"America doesn't manufacturer anything anymore** and she will make sure that we start up again".

How wrong can one person be (except of course her husband).

If she was accurate there would be no:

Boeing Corporation beating the pants off Airbus.
Apple Computer selling more I-pods and I-phones than it can produce.
No cars, wash machines, no fiber optics, no countertops or kitchen cabinets, no plumbing supplies.
No Pharmaceuticals, no farm or construction machinery. And on and on. Last year American Companies sold a huge $1.6 TRILLION in Exports.

That does not count sales here in the U.S.

Hillary, Hillary, wherefore art thou ?!?

A Twelve Year Search and Investigation!

MEDICARE & PRESCRIPTION DRUGS:

*T*he media, the liberal AARP and liberal politicians slammed the new Medicare drug program for seniors *right from the very beginning* and we continue to see negative comments, although fewer, because many have seen the truth. *This new program is great!* Unfortunately, many seniors at the beginning of the program became brainwashed by the media, AARP and the Democrats into thinking that it was a horrendous, un-workable program.

A big majority (near 90%) of seniors are now saving hundreds and even thousands of dollars on their prescriptions. *Most all eligible seniors* have become part of the new program. *A huge success!* Many even *get drugs free,* especially generic drugs or for a few dollar co-payment, and with little (less than .50 cents a day) or no monthly premiums. *How good is that?*

Unfortunately, many seniors are not capable of making choices and learning about all the great plans out there. They need family or friends to help them! Same way there are agencies helping seniors with their taxes at no cost. Because of so many similar but different programs out there, it is confusing, but, there are many aids and many independent insurance agents are happy to come to your house and sit down with you and your family.

There are also federal, state and drug company programs that will give free or low cost drugs to those who are in real need! But remember, many seniors need help in discovering these great programs. Family, friends, pharmacists, social workers, doctors, Government agencies, etc., offer assistance. Seniors *and their families and friends have to search and ask advice! There is never a dumb question!*

New private Medicare health programs offered by Insurance Companies, in place of and paid by Medicare, can save lots of dollars. My wife and I both have one of the new programs which is free (your Medicare payment to the government pays the premium). We no longer need a Medicare supplement, which cost nearly $2,000 annually in the past. We now just pay a small co-pay for a doctor office visit, ($5.00), nothing for lab work, and can only be charged *a very maximum* of $2,000 in any one year *regardless of the serious medical* problems one could have. Also*, a maximum* of $150 for a hospital visit regardless of *how long you are in.* Many extras are included like *preventive type* programs that are not available in regular Medicare only.

A big saving, yet we both go frequently for various ailments like heart, arthritis, pacemaker, blood pressure, etc. To be on the safe side, we now put that savings (the old monthly payment for a supplement), in a special account for emergency use, (that we probably will never need)!

As we are on the subject of Seniors and Medicare, etc., we should report about the possible use of stem cell research. Our local Diocesan weekly newspaper, recently had a very revealing story *about the fallacies* in embryonic stem cell research. Written by Fr. Tadeusz Pacholczyk, who is director of education at the National Catholic Bioethics Center in Philadelphia. Father *has a doctorate in neuroscience from Yale.* (www.ncbcenter.org). Our thanks to Fr. Pacholczyk for allowing us to use his theory!

Supposedly, there are about 400,000 frozen human embryos. Perhaps, the radical, liberal Katie Couric put is most bluntly in an interview with White House aide, Karen Hughes. Couric said, *"Of course, many of these frozen embryos will be discarded because they won't be needed, so they'll be thrown in a "DUMPSTER" anyway. Does it trouble President Bush that these "THINGS" are being "THROWN AWAY" when they have the potential to save lives?"*

Unfortunately, this widely reported argument has ensnared many commentators, lawmakers, Americans and many Catholics.

The vast majority *will not be* "thrown away" as approximately **88% are kept for their original use.** *Only about 2.2%* have been have been designated for disposal. *Only 2.8% are designated for research* which leaves about 11,000. Again, another real problem: It takes anywhere from *15 to 20 embryos to get one success.* Which leaves *only several hundred useable,* which is way to small to create any significant, measurable treatment.

The real problem will be what this may lead to down the road (which is well on the way). Much care must be taken or we could go down the wrong roads!

Seniors also receive many other great benefits like meals-on-wheels, senior centers in most communities offering a variety of services from low cost meals to entertainment trips to free health screenings like blood pressure, eyes, hearing, etc., and low cost or free transportation services to doctors, shopping, etc. Many cities now have free clinics for those who cannot afford to go to a doctor or hospital. Many restaurants and retail stores also offer some great discounts for seniors. Utilities will help with heating for the poor.

It's possible for seniors at one local chain buffet restaurant outlet to get a great choice of fresh fruits, vegetables, salads, entrees, dessert, beverages, for $4.95. **First run movies** are available for seniors on Friday afternoons for $3.75 at one local theatre (they also have discounted popcorn and soda -- for seniors only). One discount (second run) theatre has $1.50 movies on Tuesdays. Most all YMCA's and their type of private businesses, have great programs for seniors at reduced rates.

It has become *easier and easier* to have a great life as a senior *regardless of* what the **liberal democrats and the media tell** the nation with their *usual scare tactics*. Anything to win the next election!!

What are YOU going to do about it?

CUTS IN EDUCATION:

Another myth perpetuated by the liberals.

Education funds the last 5 years *have increased an* average of 9% per year from $36 Billion to *$90 Billion in 2007.* The same with student loans (Pell Grants), from near *$8 Billion to over $13 Billion for 2008.* The highest available Pell Grant loan was also increased for the first time in years, up to $4,600 per year. Which could pay about ¾ of the average state college tuition and expenses around the country. The average loan was about $2,350. Only those *with incomes of under $50,000* are eligible and most loans in the Pell grant program *go to those under $20,000.*

The administration has now undertaken the huge task of cutting the fraud and abuse in all these programs and increasing slightly the interest costs to the recipients in an effort to make them more efficient to decrease the budget to save all Americans taxes. (Of course the liberals *call this a cut in education* funding and may reverse this interest increase to students in the next session of Congress). More brainwashing! (See the section on No Child Left Behind).

A Twelve Year Search and Investigation!

Another *liberal myth* that should be looked at, charges, that low income students are not able to get into colleges or universities. *Very wrong!* New studies show that *the percentage of high school students entering college varies little by income.* Example: *53.3%* of those with *incomes under $16,800* get into college. Compare *this to 65.1%* of those with incomes from $18,600 to $80,000. Where is the big, huge discrepancy? It is not there! Sure there is a difference, but take a look at the underlining reasons which most likely show that the upper income students are better prepared, have better incentives and are just more motivated with better opportunities.

It is now reported that *only 35% of high school* seniors are proficient in reading and *only 23%* proficient in math. 40% of those can't read above a 2'nd grade level. An additional new study determined that only 50% of *college graduates* are proficient in reading and math.

James Simon, President of Renaissance Technology Corporation, when speaking to the National Governors Association, reported many math and science teachers now in our schools, do not know the subject matter. Why? Very simple! Those who know

What are YOU going to do about it?

the subject can start at near $100,000 per year in business and industry but only $30,000 to $40,000 in schools. See additional student/teacher info under the study on the U.S. Moral Breakdown.

While we are on the subject of education, we should also report that new information released recently, shows *that per student cost per day is at least double* the cost of most other Western/industrialized nations. Our national average is near $10.00 per day, per student, as compared to around $5.00 average in other nations. In California in fact, it is near $15.00. Have all these *funds raised through taxes produced* a positive result?

No! We have fallen well back in most areas of math, science, engineering etc., so that we are now *near the bottom* in most of these areas compared to most other industrialized nations. Another study showed that, despite all these funds, reading scores for 9 year olds has *virtually stayed the same since 1980*. Are you aware that *1.2 million high school students drop out* each year. Oprah recently said she is fed up with trying to help those in the ghettos, as all they ask for is I-pods and sneakers. Therefore she has built a new controversial multi-million dollar school for girls in

Africa. *30 killed in Chicago schools* in the 2007-08 school year. *Near the same* in every major city!

So, we spend much more and get far less! Mostly do to un-educated or apathetic parents, liberal demands, spending habits of liberal politicians, liberal judges coddling students with politically correct rulings and liberal teacher unions demanding more in salaries and fringes but producing less & less in many areas especially the coastal areas. The federal government *doles out $40 Billion for K-12 school* systems each year. (YES, Billions)! Yet we hear liberals continually badgering the administration and congress for more. We are doing something awfully wrong when 2/3 of high school graduates can't do college level work.

If education results improved dramatically, most citizens would be happy to pay a bit more. We also see that most schools in America's heartland are in great condition, but schools in the liberal big cities are falling apart. Is this a federal problem, or should these liberal, big cities, look at their own problems of taxation and funding for schools at the local level as we do in mid-America where we have respect for good education? It should be noted that big cities

---

What are YOU going to do about it?

have expensive crime and drug enforcement problems that are far less in middle America!

Also recently, several publications looked at liberal educators at the college level. They found that there are many *former terrorist sympathizers or fugitives* wanted or under surveillance by the FBI that have, or are, teaching in our Universities. *(Read: "The Professors -- The 101 Most Dangerous Academics in America," by David Horowitz and/or refer to the "2006 Campus Outrage Awards" published in the "Collegiate Network" on Monday, April 3, 2006. You'll find these articles very revealing).*

Also found was that a huge percentage of professors are strictly *radically liberal* in their politics and very anti-administration. Some recent national stories about *two really radical, psychotic professors* in Colorado and Wisconsin has shown how serious this problem really is. Unfortunately, many bring their liberal teachings into the *classrooms,* brainwashing students. Many interviews with students have verified this.

Your taxes are paying for the federal government giving near *$80 Billion in federal grants to colleges* and universities. State governments chip in another $70 Billion. It now takes *twice as many professors* and staff to man these institutions as a decade ago.

Many Universities now have huge indoor recreation areas with huge aquatic areas, climbing walls, massages available, movies, live entertainment, etc., costing millions and millions. We have turned many of *them into luxury country clubs* competing against private entertainment and service enterprises. Tuitions of $40,000 to $50,000 and up per year!

Many professors spend a great deal of time on research *(with little transparency)* and very little teaching. Unfortunately, professors have tenure and the institution administrations find it very difficult to remove them, even after being charged, indicted or *convicted of serious crimes*, (some even getting salaries while serving jail time), and some for child molestation or *sex crimes against students.* Our *radical, liberal teacher unions and University faculty* groups are the reasons for very little prosecution!!

16% of the public have no high school diploma!!! 70% of Detroit students fail to graduate from High school. It is near 50% in most large cities.

What are YOU going to do about it?

Interesting thoughts on going GREEN !!

There is a mansion in the South with separate guest house, 20 rooms, 8 baths, heated pool and pool house, all heated with natural gas. Average electricity and gas monthly is near $2,400. This property consumes more than 20 times what the average house consumes!

Another house is 4,000 sq. ft., 4 bedrooms. A central closet in the house holds geothermal heat-pumps drawing water 300 feet from under ground. The water is a constant 67 degrees and heats and cools the house year round. All waste water and rain water is saved, purified then used to water plants, shrubs, lawns, etc. The house uses no fossil fuels and only ¼ the electricity of the average house.

The first house above belongs to environmentalist Al Gore outside of Nashville.

The second house belongs to President Bush in Crawford, Texas.

Who's the real environmentalist? Another MYTH?

A Twelve Year Search and Investigation!

NO CHILD LEFT BEHIND:

Doing great in many cities and states in spite of media, liberals and NEA fighting it at every turn! *Plenty of money if used according to the federal rules* and regulations! (But not according to the liberal teacher unions and media)! They would rather attack and fight the President on every issue!

Instead of helping our children get a good education, they would rather win the next elections regardless of any consequences! *Just bash the President* and claim the program is useless! *The public is brainwashed* frequently by the liberal media quoting teacher union representatives and interviews on TV and using them for commentaries in local papers.

Teacher unions have always fought a system of ratings for teachers or schools and made it very difficult *to eliminate inefficient teachers*, etc. Many attempts have been made to rate teachers according to performance. It's always attacked and usually *blocked by the unions.* School boards are helpless and frustrated in trying to do the right thing with curriculum, salaries, keeping the best teachers, etc.

What are YOU going to do about it?

SOCIAL SECURITY:

*W*here do the liberals expect to get billions, starting in 2017, **and increasing every year after,** when SS takes in less than it is paying out and those retiring double in numbers, making it necessary to make up the deficit in Social Security. The money has been borrowed from Social Security and **spent by our** government and will have to come from somewhere like increase in taxes, cuts in service, etc., in order to repay the Social Security trust fund and have the funds necessary to keep the current levels of social security payments to our seniors.

All these problems were started by Democrats over the years when **they, the Democrats**, voted to allow the government to put the SS tax money in the general fund. **Then they, the liberal Democrats**, also decided to tax SS as seniors income.

There is no "lockbox", no money, yet, the liberals continue to fight the President and refuse to take action to correct this very large looming problem! Action now may help later. More obstruction!

A Twelve Year Search and Investigation!

It has now been estimated that the three major entitlement programs, Social Security, Medicare and Medicaid *will take up 80% of the total federal budget* within the next 15 years or so. But, Democrats continue *to obstruct any solutions!*

The only solution is to privatize for those under 45 or so, or drastically cut monthly S.S. payments, higher co-pays for prescription drugs, cut Medicaid or raise premiums for Medicare. Those above 45 or so would *not be affected* and would get what's been promised. But those under that would have the option of putting *a portion* of their premium into a fund similar to what teachers use or Congress uses that would give them back a big interest increase based on past history.

Now, the social security program pays about .8% interest and maybe not even that if you die sooner than later (you may never get any back if you have an early death). If available, the privatized portion would be yours to use as you please and would go to your survivors and not taken by the government. It could pay from 2% to up to 9% or more depending on the economy. It relieves the government of some of the costs associated with the normal way.

What are YOU going to do about it?

Obama and the Rev. Wright fabrication:

Frequently Barack Obama has mislead the public on the background of the Rev. Wright. He continually talked about the Rev. having to remember the reality of his generation and the humiliation and fear, the anger and bitterness of those years.

In reality, the Rev. grew up in a racially mixed, middle class neighborhood with broad tree lined streets and his father a pastor and his mother a vice-principle of a high school for girls. Both had good jobs and Wright was able to attend a 90% white, elite privileged high school. No ghetto and no lack of opportunity.

He was well respected by the students and described as the "epitome of what Central endeavors to imbue in its students".

Bill Crosby also attended and has since denounced the black culture of victim hood that Wright promotes in his sermons. A culture that Crosby says sets up blacks for failure.

The media has refused to explain and have anointed Obama as the Democrat "beauty pageant nominee".

A Twelve Year Search and Investigation!

CHAPTER III

GLOBAL WARMING:

*M*any prominent scientists, (not just a few as per Gore) who have all the information from hundreds, even thousands of years at their finger tips, have said *repeatedly,* that, at the moment, there is global warming which is normal, and caused simply by the *normal ups and downs of weather patterns* going back hundreds of years.

Not to many years ago, there was a hew and cry about a cold pattern (here in Wisconsin's Fox Valley we had 6 inches of snow on May 6 back in the 40's and for many years there were periods of 20 to 30 below zero many days in a row—*HEY, I LIVED THROUGH IT!)* and it was reported that the ice-age may be returning unless we do something about it (as reported by the NY Times).

The near record heat of the summer of '06 was still not enough to break the record held in 1936 (obviously, it must have been global warming then too----right?). And do we remember *the "dust bowl" days back in the 30's.* All *reported by the N.Y. Times*, at the time, as global warming.

But the liberal press continues to stir up the public when some wacky college professor, a Hollywood liberal with no expertise or Gore (and his new movie) warns us that the world is coming to an end unless things change. (We should remember that Gore did "invent the internet".... SURE! He also flunked out of two grad schools and barely graduated high school with very poor grades). It has also been reported that he does little to help the environment in his private life, keeping up two huge homes. One home is reported to use as much energy in one month than the average home uses in a year.

Gore when speaking about his movie, "An Inconvenient Truth", said, "I believe *it is appropriate* to have an *over-representation* of factual presentations on how dangerous global warming **could be**"...In other words...***EXAGGERATE*** !! Newly released information and investigations by *"real"* experts are showing that most of Gore's claims are *fabrications and highly exaggerated* as he himself indicated.

Gore also testified that all, over 1,000 scientists, agreed that it was indeed as he had said it was, Global Warming and a serious problem. Not true! 120 nations were represented at the U.N. European meeting but *there were few atmospheric scientists* and *mostly* just un-elected bureaucrats (who had a tough time coming to a consensus).

A professor emeritus of the atmospheric department at Colorado State University and America's most reliable hurricane forecaster, has said that Gore is one of those guys preaching the end of the world type things and that he is doing a great *disservice* and doesn't know what he is talking about!

He also said that fluctuations in hurricane intensities has nothing to do with carbon dioxide levels or human activity but with natural variations in ocean currents. We can't blame humans or CO2.

The average temperature dropped 5 degrees between 1902 and 1910 because of thick ash and dust clouds from volcanic eruptions and a comet striking Siberia. In Greenland, the little ice age came around the year 1400 and temperatures declined by 2.7 degrees and advancing glaciers doomed the Viking Colony to global cooling. Swiss scientists believe that glaciers in the *Alps have melted away at least ten times* in the past 10,000 years.

Researchers at the Max Planck Institute in Germany report that the sun has been burning more brightly over the past 100 years accounting for the 1 degree increase. A geology professor from Washington University, also notes that within the last 15,000 years, there *has been shifts* up to "20 times greater than the warming of the past century".

Another interesting observation shows that the number of Sunspots on the Suns surface caused by magnetic fields, have a 11 year cycle. Ironically, at the very same time, *the Earths temperature corresponds to these ups ands downs.* The graph on the next page (page 69) shows this very dramatically. At the same time, CO_2 concentrations, while rising, are very straight lined and *have little dramatic ups and downs* to correspond to the variances in temperature. There *appears to be little or no relation.*

While we are no experts, as are most who give opinions on the subject of Global Warming, we all must look at all possible reasons for this new highly publicized nationally discussed phenom.

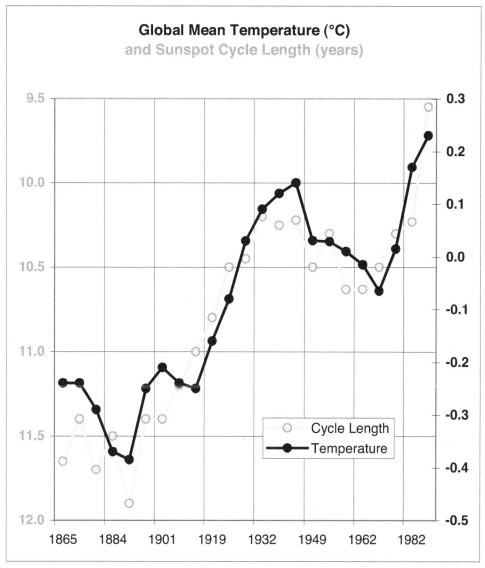

Another myth perpetuated by the global warning alarmists continue to tell Southern California residents that the air quality is far worse now than 40 years ago. A complete falsehood. 40 years ago residents were forced to stay inside for several days *nearly every week,* but now it only happens several *times a year.*

It is very clear to most everyone that something has to be done on the energy level by the federal government. All our Senators and Representatives keep talking about it in Congress, but nothing much gets done. *We must become energy independent from the rest of world.*

More myths!!! Hurricanes are more intense and do more damage now. Wrong! There are 50% more people living in Florida and most Gulf states than years ago. Many are richer and have better and more expensive homes and more extravagant belongings, etc. This creates up to 500% more costly damage. Nothing to do with Global Warming.

More malaria because of Global Warming !!! Wrong! Only in poor countries. Not in countries with means to fight it. Not Global Warming.

Let's take a look at some possible, perhaps radical, but perhaps doable, solutions *that just might work:*

All **new** homes **built after 2020,** must be 50% or better, self sufficient for all energy needs. Using wind, solar, construction methods and materials including the new straw-bale and earth-plaster method, and similar, etc.

All new cars, vans, suv's, light pick-ups, must have combination electric, gas, or other alternative fuels and get at least 50 miles per gallon by 2020.

All new farm machinery, run by fuels or electricity must become 40% more efficient by 2030.

Manufacturers using petroleum products, electricity, natural gas, etc., must be 40% more efficient by 2030.

All governments offices, Congress, federal agencies, etc., using energy, must reduce use by 50% using solar, wind, nuclear, etc., by 2025.

Any manufactured products made with petroleum products, must use other methods instead of petroleum for manufacturing by 2025.

80% of all petroleum products sold or used in the U.S. must come from U.S. produced petroleum by 2040.

What are YOU going to do about it?

Existing homes, condos, apartments, etc., must become 20% more efficient by 2020, 30% by 2030.

All *new* retail, manufacturing, office buildings must be 40% energy self sufficient after 2020.

All existing retail buildings must become 40% more energy efficient by 2020.

Using nuclear, water power and solar combined with additional oil from the Gulf, Alaska, West Coast would make us self-dependent and eliminate any need for foreign oil purchases and also along with most of the above by 2025. Hey, I was the only one I know that called the 2007-08 Packer season totals on the mark. Maybe some cannot be done. **What are your ideas?**

HURRICANE KATRINA:

Another example of brainwashing by the liberals and media! The Louisiana Governor failed to respond with the National Guard in a timely fashion leaving much of the area un-protected and no one to help those in need (the President and FEMA called her many times wondering when she was going to act). Much of the city police force did not report and were AWOL fleeing their hometown they were to protect.

The mayor, *according to previous plan*, was to use 100's of school busses to get the poor and medically impaired out of the city and failed to do it. Previous mayors had used the Superdome for the same type emergency but had water, food, cots, generators and portable toilets available. *This mayor had none!*

In fact, it was reported that the mayor hid in a hotel room for several days after the storm, afraid to face the public or answer to federal authorities, as he didn't have a clue on how to handle the situation. But the media jumped on the President and FEMA from *the first day even though he or they had nothing to do* with the problems in the first few days.

What are YOU going to do about it?

Meanwhile, several *big huge hotels had all* the generators, food and supplies they needed to stay in business but hospitals and the city not. Why? FEMA and the Federal Government is usually for clean-up, not emergency first response *until summoned by local authorities.* The President called the Governor the Sunday before and she reported "we're in good shape!" President: "Our assets are available to you".

Of course, we should mention that the Hurricane was so massive, that no government agency could have been ready for something like that. Same if a severe earthquake or atomic bomb hit New York or Chicago and destroyed it. *Some things cannot be planned for.*

We also continually hear or read the liberals and press complaining that the federal government had failed to respond with little funding. *Very wrong.* The President announced early on, that well near $120 Billion has been approved for clean-up and rebuilding.

The problem lies in that city and state governments failed to complete a plan for reconstruction and failed *to apply for the funds that just sat there* waiting to be used (at their discretion). Meanwhile, the State of *Mississippi was nearly back to normal.* Hmmmmm....

A Twelve Year Search and Investigation!

POPULATION EXPLOSION

Frequently we hear a hue and cry about the U.S. becoming over populated. While a few areas in the nation have problems and several third world countries and others nations have problems, statistical information about the U. S. is not alarming at this time.

Consider that the U.S. has the third largest population (300 million) as compared to China at 1.3 billion and India 1.1 billion.

On a list of population density, the U. S. ranks 143 out of 193. The world's density is 43 people per square kilometer and the U.S. is 30. Ironically, many countries who have very active green space environmental laws much more stringent than the U.S., yet have more serious problems. Among major countries who are highest the Netherlands with 395, Belgium 337, Great Britain 233, Germany 230, Italy 190, Switzerland 180, Denmark 126, France 111.

Other worse areas are Singapore and Hong Kong with about 6,300, Taiwan 630, South Korea 491 and

---

What are YOU going to do about it?

Monaco with a huge 16,610. While the U.S. is one of fastest growing because of immigration, birth rate and longevity increase, we are one of the few western industrialized countries *that are not going the other* way. *Losing* population!

Historically, before the 20th Century, the majority of Americans lived in small cities, towns and rural area. Now, an amazing *80% live in highly populated big city* metropolitan areas. The population sprawl in not the result of population growth. *Home size* is at record highs, many now have *second and third homes* and *more people have homes* than ever before. In addition the divorce revolution has created millions **of double households.** An ever growing number also live alone and these numbers are projected to increase in the future.

Bob Hope:
"Give me the sense of humor, Lord, give me the grace to see a joke, to get some humor out of life and to pass it on to other folks".

HEATING HOMES:

*A*nother easily solved problem. I believe the average increase in home heating 2006 amounted to about $300 for a family (give or take a $100). Again, not much more than the cost of a cup of coffee per day (or about .80 cents or less)! But the liberals and media continually sent out the scare tactic releases that the public is going to go broke or lose their homes, etc., etc.

My wife and I (both retired) simply turned our thermostat down a couple of degrees and dressed a little warmer and saw very little change from the year before. A solvable problem!

How many people take advantage of the free help available from your power companies in suggesting how to save on energy? But the media and liberals were screaming for the government *to pay* the increase or *take it* from the energy companies profits. More socialism! Not necessary!!

What are YOU going to do about it?

Recently, George Will, respected journalist, reported that Michille Obama said, "Most Americans' lives have gotten progressively worse since I was a little girl." (She was born in 1964).

Since 1960: per capita income up 143%!
 Life expectancy up seven years!
 Infant Mortality down 74%!
 Heart disease deaths cut in half!
 Depression has become treatable!
 Air and water pollution down dramatically!
 Women with Bachelor Degrees over double!
 Home ownership up 10.2%!
 Home size has more than doubled!
 Homes with Air up from 12% to 77%!
 Americans with stock ownership quintupled!
 The Obamas income last year: $4.2 million!
 20% of those with incomes under $50,000 paid
  Capital Gains taxes in 2006.
 A few decades ago, 1 in 10 Blacks were in the
  Middle class---now 1 in 3!!
 How many countries have complete Freedom
  Of Religion, Speech, etc., etc.
 Millions more seniors, are now
  investing in the Stock Market.
 30% now have degrees–only 7% two decades ago.

I can't imagine how she could stand all that? AMAZING!

A Twelve Year Search and Investigation!

PRICE GOUGING

When I was a kid in the 30's gas was selling for $.20 per gallon. Five for a buck! Now gas is up about 15 times. *But look at these:*

Movie was .10 cents--- -now up **70 times** or so.
New car for less than $700 ---- **now 20 times.**
Ice cream cones a nickel --- now **40 times** or so.
Popcorn at a movie was .10 --- now **36 times.**
New 5-bed house for $4,000 --- now **50 times.**
French fries for .05 --- now **20 times** or so.
Hamburger for .10 --- now **20 times** or so.
Hamburger at the meat market for **.20 per pound.**

You can figure your own rent, utilities, phones, etc.

According to Morgan Stanley they estimate that the cost of finding and *developing oil is three times* greater today than just back in 1999.

Who's doing the gouging? No one! It's a free market. That's what brings immigrants here. The American dream!! Everyone is eligible! Gasoline would have to

---

What are YOU going to do about it?

increase to $3.50 or more per gallon to get up to the rate of inflation.

Did you know oil companies have increased their investment in Exploration and Production from less than $60 Billion in 2002 to over $120 Billion in 2006?

The percentage of profits for oil companies *was easily surpassed* by many other business groups: Oil company profits were at **9%** for the 3'rd quarter of 2006. But look at Pharmaceuticals **21%**, Beverages and Tobacco **19%**, Electrical Equipment **14%**, Chemicals **13%**, Computers **11%**. Average for all manufacturing **8.4%**. All doing well *because of the great economy.*

Gas price percent of increase from early 80's to 2005 was 90% (about 25 years). But again various industries: Tuition, school fees and childcare, 325% increase. Medical care, 220%. Rent, 110%. Food, 85%.

(Statistics from the U.S. Energy Information Administration, Oil Company reports, Manufacturing Associations, etc. The statistics at the top came from my own personal experiences as a boy of 11 or 12. I was born in 1928. Housing costs came from various internet sources).

A Twelve Year Search and Investigation!

GAS PRICES:

*T*he liberals and the liberal media continually rant that the President is to blame for energy prices going up. The liberal Democrats in Congress, led by radical environmentalists have continually fought the President at every turn for an energy bill for many years. *They refuse to allow* DEEP SEA ENERGY EXPLORATION in the gulf and the west coast of the U. S. Part of *Alaska is, and always been,* out of bounds by liberals.

Liberal, activist environmentalists and democrats **continued** to **prevent** most any administration initiative in the energy area including alternative *energy like wind, water, and nuclear.* The *public wants* these desperately and keeps saying so in many polls, but *not in my backyard.* So, proposed developers are *blocked by local citizens* regularly after brainwashing *by environmentalists.* Much of what they preach is utterly nonsense or over-stated, but the old saying, *"say it enough and some will believe"!*

When gas prices reached over $3.00 per gallon we continually heard the doom and gloom of the press and TV when reporting on gas prices. "Draining our pocketbooks", was a favorite phrase used on TV, but, when analyzed, *we found that the average person* in middle America, *with an average car*, driving 25 miles per day or so, or living within about 10-12 miles of their job (MOST DO OR COULD), only spent about the *cost of a soda at a convenience store* in additional daily expenses. *90% drive less than 30 miles per day!*

Meanwhile, most average citizens have no problems with the higher prices. We can eliminate seniors, most of whom are retired (millions) and need to do little driving. Most anyone earning over $70,000, or above, (millions) should have no problem with the minor extra cost. Then there are millions of teens and college kids with little need to drive many miles. (All *of these account for well over 3/4 of our citizens)*
.

The biggest areas of problems are in the big cities *who have not kept up* with growing transportation gridlock, but many have excellent public transportation which millions use and many more could use. Even here in Wisconsin's Fox Valley, we have good public transportation or can use a bike or walk. Most grocery and other shopping is well with-in

A Twelve Year Search and Investigation!

most citizens' easy reach in middle America. Most within a 5 or 10 minute drive.

At the same time we hear the vulnerable general public complaining about gas prices, *(simply repeating what they hear on TV daily).* Brainwashed. We *see millions of these* same vulnerable citizens gambling **daily** in casinos and on the internet, **buying** lottery tickets, **paying** $6.00 or more for a beer, $4.00 or more for a hotdog and $3.75 for a soda at a professional sports game, *or several times a day* **buying** a small bottle of water at a convenience store at a cost of $10.00 or more, (per gallon cost)! *All rich people buying these products??* Hardly!

Just look at the **average** Joe at convenience stores buying huge sodas, water, snacks, etc., (are the rich only buying this stuff), daily expensive latte or cappuccinos for several dollars, many still smoking (several dollars a day), eating out often, (seems like all restaurants are full every lunch hour and try to get a table on Friday or Saturday night or Sunday morning).

Much of the public discontent can be attributed to *media over-blowing the problem.* One TV station on *every newscast* shows a screen filling report on the

---

What are YOU going to do about it?

cost of gas in each city in the area. Even when there is no change for weeks at a time. They just keep brainwashing! *National TV news programs* will show daily, the highest price and lowest price of the day, throughout the country.

Movie attendance is up with many standing in line buying buckets of popcorn for over $5.00 and soda for $4.00. Close to $10.00 to get in the movie. *Again, are they all rich??* Far from it!

Parents and kids on their cell-phones, computers or I-Pods and purchasing huge plasma HD televisions with surround sound speakers and many families driving their big SUV's and trucks, *(are all rich???)*, but all the time complaining that they are being robbed by the gas companies, *(repeating the propaganda they hear every day).* The middle class is growing and not really being hurt by gas prices and they are *getting richer because of the great economy!*

Recently, Our Performing Arts Center here in our city of near 75,000, brought in Disney's broadway production of "Lion King" It played for six weeks and filled every night. At near $75.00 per ticket. *Only* the rich? Hardly!

A Twelve Year Search and Investigation!

OIL COMPANY PROFITS:

*T*he oil companies have had excellent profits but not nearly *as large as many other industries.* One example, during one of the last quarters in 2006, McDonalds announced *an increase in profits of 57%.*

The *huge Time Warner, had a 60% profit increase* in a quarter lately, with profits *of $1.46 Billion,* whereas, Exxon U. S. sales profit were about $1.6 Billion, (but one has to remember *they, Exxon, is the world's largest* corporation). *Do we see the press or liberals going* after McDonalds or Time Warner (who increases their cable rates every year), and *have had much larger* percentage of profits? Or the many other companies who also had huge profits (*because of the great economy)!*

Most companies in fact reported excellent profits **not reported by the major media.** In fact, the average percentage of profit for all companies was about 8.6% nation-wide. *Exxon was below average at 8.4%.*

And only a few years ago the energy companies were *losing money* -- it takes billions and many years of

What are YOU going to do about it?

planning to build and expand refineries or explore for new energy sources. But Democrats and radical *environmentalists continually obstruct all efforts* and make it *nearly impossible, taking years,* to get the necessary government and public support and permits. **Oil companies** paid nearly $100 **billion** in taxes in 2007

Another favorite talking point in the liberal media and Democrats, suggested that people couldn't afford to go on vacation and had to cut back. *Ridiculous and completely unfounded!* And most people realized that, (but yet the *media continued to play* it up....again, *anything to embarrass the President)!!*

Going a hundred miles or so from home to a resort for example, cost about $25.00 for gas (give or take a buck or two), but then stayed several days or more in a fancy resort or motel paying $100 to $300 or more per night, plus food and entertainment, spending *perhaps 5 or 6 hundred or even much more for a couple of nights vacation or maybe even thousands if it's a week or more.*

Obviously the gas price of the vacation *was a very small percentage* of the total cost. It is also interesting that the price of gas in Spring 2007, nearly reached its all time high when considering inflation ($3.50 or more)! More proof: Door County Wisconsin tourism, one of the main tourist areas in the Midwest, *was near* normal in 2006!!!

But when it is suggested to the public that a smaller car would help or car-pooling or consolidating their shopping trips, etc., most of the public wants no part of it! "I want my SUV or truck"!!!

How many kids drove their cars to school years ago in the good old days? ***None!*** Now look at the parking lots and surrounding streets at all our high schools! *FULL* to capacity! How many families had 2 or 3 cars and garages to put them in back *in grandma's days*?

And look at the parking lots at work, at church, picking up kids at school or mall areas -- you see a ***big majority*** of pick-up trucks, vans and suv's (the most expensive transportation). Many are also seen towing campers and/or boats, snowmobiles, etc. Is it just the rich who go hunting or fishing, golfing, memberships at the Y, attending professional sports events in record numbers, etc.? Not hardly!! **All rich** *people? Again, far from it!*

During world war II'

The Russion lost an average

of 3,000 soldiers per day

during one period of the war.

BUT:
2 per day in Iraq!

CHAPTER IV

WORLD OPINION:

*I*nterestingly, the liberal media and democrats have always accused the President of ruining our relationships with the rest of the world. Now, in 2007, we see that Germany, France, Canada and soon England and Spain will have elected new *pro-Bush leaders*. Now isn't that a turn around?

There are also dozens of reason why the radical Muslim world and a few European countries have grown to despise us but many seem to be having second thoughts. We are making inroads! *Here are the top five reasons and none caused by President Bush:*

(1) The U. S. support for Israel going back many decades is huge.

(2) Our declining morals broadcast world wide by media and Hollywood films and TV. In late 2007, the " Law and Order" TV series, had anti-American, anti-

Government, anti-administration themes. Liberal to the core!   There are others!

(3) Liberal Democrats, European and U.S. media and Hollywood celebrities all bashing the President *daily* and reported *worldwide* by the European and Muslim press.

(4) Obstructionist statements by some foreign leaders in the U.N. when debating the Iraq invasion (and then finding *out they were getting oil payback money* under the table from Saddam).

(5) Horrendous TV reports of minor U.S. prisoner atrocities by international media! All started by the liberal *U.S. press leaking stories and over-blowing them.*

Nothing the President did! More brainwashing!!

We also continue to see in the press and by liberal democrats, that the President caused the hatred between the Arab communities and the U.S. **Very wrong!!** As I mention later in this book, (under Terrorism), most of this hatred started *nearly 3 decades ago,* long before Bush took office, when the

Iranians took over the U. S. Embassy in Iran and kept hostages for many months (*under President Carter*).

This was followed for many years by dozens of suicide bombings in Israel by Muslim radicals killing hundreds of innocent citizens in malls, pizza parlors, etc. *Many airliners* were hijacked and/or blasted out of the sky.

Olympic athletes from Israel were kidnapped and killed, the *first World Trade Center bombing in N.Y.*, killing 241 U. S. Marines in Biruit, the bombings of several U.S. Embassies and the USS Cole, many kidnappings of citizens *plus Saddam, for over 12 years,* ignored the U.N.'s many resolutions and refused to cooperate as he killed hundred of thousands of his own citizens with *WMD's* and invaded two of his neighboring countries!

Are you following this? *None under President Bush!!*

Terrorist leader bin Ladin was responsible for much of this terrorism under the previous Clinton administration including the planning of 9-11 (several years before it happened).

What are YOU going to do about it?

All before the President Bush took office!!!

Of course, if we would have done what some liberal Democrats want to do, (do not invade Iraq---after they voted to remove Saddam), all this would have continued without recourse of any kind and Saddam would still be killing thousands every year and the Taliban, Al Qaeda and bin Ladin would still be operating in full view. Under Clinton the U.S. had little response, although Clinton frequently promised to get the terrorists, he and his Attorney General reportedly passed up numerous opportunities to get bin Ladin.

They were too busy going after Bill Gates and Microsoft.

COALITIONS:

"We went into Iraq alone"! False! *9 countries invaded with us on the ground!* Eventually near *45 or more nations*, with near 30,000 troops and billions in aid, (actually a bigger coalition than the first desert storm war). But not according to the liberals! More brainwashing as they continually report (*AND STILL DO*) we went in alone. Soldiers from Spain, Italy, Poland, England, Netherlands, Bulgaria, Hungary, Australia *and others have been killed in Iraq*.

It took Germany and Japan nearly 10 years to accept us after WWII and we still have thousands of troops there (after 60 years)!

The liberals also contend that we left Afghanistan too early. *We never really left*, (not entirely, as we kept 10,000 to 30,000 troops there), much of the Afghanistan security efforts was taken over by *coalition forces led by NATO* with a dozen or more countries and the emerging, newly trained Afghanistan army and police security forces. *We did not abandon* them as frequently mentioned by liberals.

What are YOU going to do about it?

Please!
A LITTLE PERSPECTIVE!!!

WE LOST MORE
in one day
ON 9-11

THAN
U.S. SOLDIERS
IN FOUR YEARS
IN IRAQ!!!!!

INTELLIGENCE GATHERING:

*D*isgruntled former liberal CIA employees "blew the whistle" and accused the President of secret domestic spying and leaked it to the New York Times.

Although it was well explained by the administration that the surveillance *only included calls from overseas by suspected terrorists* to some one in the U.S., or vice-versa, the liberals and media were quick to pounce on their new found toy, *blatantly and falsely* accusing the administration of spying on Americans in their homes, *(with no proof),* just to discredit the President (even though what they were really doing was perfectly legal according to the Attorney General, several federal Judges, several Supreme Court Justices, the Federal War Crimes Act and the President's authority as Commander-in-Chief).

(The Liberals have made the surveillance act one of *over 300 investigations* and hearings by the Senate and House in 2007, trying *to find or drum up* "*something*" *to* "*get*" the current, "*other side of the aisle*", and turn the public against the Conservatives.

What are YOU going to do about it?

Anything to win an election. All 300 are very political motivated *and have very little substance).*

The reporting and printing this story by the New York Times, after being told by the administration not to print this secret information, turned out to be very a *serious threat to our safety* and several terrorist cells reportedly changed their methods of operation. These former employees and the Times in 2006 were *undergoing federal investigation* for exposing secret government information and informing our enemies thereby compromising national security. A very *serious offense* in wartime!

Of course, and as usual, the media again failed to report on how most all former Democratic Presidents have *done similar intelligence gathering* and in fact much more serious. FDR, Kennedy, Carter and Clinton all had secret spying of *not only enemy calls but also domestic calls.* It was *routine and widely reported* by the Times and other media as being perfectly legal, necessary and expected. Have you heard this from the nations media? *Double standard?* You guessed it!!!! *Has anyone heard of "9-11"?*

Interestingly, the liberal democrats who fought the President on this surveillance by the intelligence agencies and continually accused the administration of profiling at airports because they wanted to make sure all airport workers were citizens, etc., all of a sudden, *started profiling on their own*, when the administration reported that they might hire an Arab firm to run our ports in the U.S. (A very professional firm who was very experienced and creditable). The liberals quickly and loudly *said we can't do that, "they are Arabs"*. (Even though many European and Arab countries are managers and owners of many business and industrial firms here in the U.S. and other countries). *What goes around, comes around!*

PLEASE A LITTLE PERSPECTIVE!

*WE LOST (ON AVERAGE)
OVER 250 of our military
EVERY DAY FOR 4 YEARS
IN WORLD WAR II !*

*BUT !!
AN AVERAGE OF 2 PER DAY
IN IRAQ IN 4 YEARS !!!!*

THINK ABOUT IT !!

CHAPTER V

NATIONAL GUARD DEPLOYMENT:

*I*n the 8 years of Clinton, Gore and their liberal friends, the military conducted 26 "operational events", *nearly 2 ½ times the number in the 30 years* prior. As of 1999, there were 265,000 American troops in 135 countries. Since the end of the first *Gulf War, the military shrunk 40% under Clinton.* Army Divisions from 18 to 10, 630,000 fewer soldiers and civilians and closed 700 military installations.

All this *supported by Democrats.* Now they, the liberal democrats, question the over-use of Guards and Reserves in Iraq. *Nothing President Bush* was responsible for.

In addition, the Air Force shrunk from 36 fighter wings to 20 while experiencing at the same time a *fourfold increase in operational commitments.* During Reagan years the Navy had 586 ships and under *Clinton it dropped to 324* and planned to go to 305. In 1999 *the Navy had 22,000 empty personnel slots.*

What are YOU going to do about it?

Also, in 1999, more than half of the B1-B's were *lacking critical parts.*

In reality, Rumsfeld and Franks put together a well motivated military force in short order. The biggest intangible, showed the Military's adoration for President Bush. Complete opposite from the hatred of Clinton by the military as he was a draft dodger and failed to support them. They genuinely adored Bush and it was a mutual.

IRAQ and WMD'S:

*H*ere are *12 true facts,* out of many reasons, why we invaded Iraq and eliminated a Hitler like dictator who *killed hundreds of thousand of his own people* and actually *threatened the whole world* with WMD's:

(1) Presidents Clinton and Bush and two Congress', (nearly unanimously *by Democrats*), voted for or agreed Saddam should be removed. *It was U.S. policy* for many years starting with Clinton.

(2) Same with the U.N. in 16 resolutions over many years. *It was Policy!!* Remove Saddam!!!

(3) Polls showed that *near 80% of U.S. citizens originally supported* removing Saddam.

(4) Intelligence agencies throughout Europe and Russia, China and

(5) the U.N. *all agreed he had WMD's. He admitted* he had them!

What are YOU going to do about it?

(6) *He had used WMD'S* on his own people and against Iran *to kill thousands.*

(7) *He hid WMD's* and told the world many times he was *going to destroy them.*

(U.N. inspectors though could not verify that he destroyed them after many years of investigation and searching with no cooperation from Saddam).

(8) *Saddam also killed, mutilated, tortured thousands* of his own people, perhaps millions, (proven after nearly **500 mass graves sites were found** and discovered videos and photos of torture chambers and testimony from many survivors).

And we are also quick to forget that:
(9) *he invaded Kuwait and Iran,* his neighbors, where

(10) he killed thousands,

(11) torched oil fields trying to destroy a huge % of *the world's oil* as we drove him out in the first desert storm war (*the U.N. STOPPING the U.S.* from going all the way INTO BAGHDAD TO REMOVE SADDAM),

(12) *raped and kidnapped thousands* of Kuwait citizens who were never found and confiscated much of any value throughout the country.

BONUS: Nearly all the Democrat leaders in the Senate, Kennedy, Kerry, Hillary Clinton, etc., *all very loudly* and *BOLDLY proclaimed* that Saddam had WMD's and would have *nuclear weapons soon, without any question,* when leading up to the war. *Looking at all of the above, how anyone can accuse the President* of misleading or lying is burying their head in the sand and in effect, *"don't confuse me with the facts"!!!*

IN ADDITION:
In President *Clinton's State of the Union message* in 1992, he said, "Saddam Hussein has spent the better part of this decade and much of his nation's wealth, not for the Iraqi people, *but on developing nuclear,* chemical and biological weapons and the missals to deliver them"! *Most all Democrats agreed with him!!!*

The Iraqi Prime Minister told the London Telegraph, "*We are uncovering evidence all the time,* that Saddam had *contacts with Al-Qaeda* and also with those contacts *responsible for the Sept. 11 attacks.*" The 9-11 Commission also reported that there was *communication between Saddam and al-Qaeda.* Once again *more liberal myths* as they keep saying that **there was no contact** between THE TERRORISTS AND SADDAM. (*It's another myth* that the administration and the President reportedly said that Saddam had something to do with 9-11—**it was never said**).

Documents and e-mails found after the initial invasion have also now shown that Saddam, in fact, *did hide WMD's or sent them to Syria* to hold. Jet fighter planes were found hidden in desert areas under sand. 500 shells that had contained poison gases were found. Like looking for a certain piece of sand in a desert. Nearly impossible to find! But they are there!

In addition, *U.N. Inspectors found networks* of laboratories, safe houses, a prison laboratory complex seemingly used for human testing in *biological agents.* Scientists' homes had useful *uranium enrichment information.* Plans were also found for advanced design *on ballistic and cruise* missiles. *All were prohibited* by U.N. resolutions.

Plus *several investigations by Congress, the 9-11 Commission and others* have *proven conclusively* that *the **President did not lie** !!* Some items relied on by the intelligence community may have been found to be not as first reported*! **But, all the facts shown above*** are more than enough to warrant the removal of Saddam. No lies!!!!

Also found in the millions of documents uncovered in Baghdad, *showed that bin Laden and al Qaeda made many phone calls to Baghdad just before the 9-11* attack. Why? Yet the liberals keep insisting that there *was no association between Iraq and bin Ladin.* Other RECOVERED documents have also *proven* this to be wrong. *But all ignored by the nations media* and liberal democrats.

Another myth continually spewed by the liberals is that the President planned the war with Iraq long before we went in. This is kind of true---- to an extent! Presidents Clinton, both the old and the new Bush, and Presidents before them, as part of their *normal activities while in office, always are planning* and have contingencies for taking care of any form of hostility that may flare up on their watch.

You'll also find in his book, reported statements by General Franks, the first commander on the ground in

Iraq, that he, the Chiefs of Staff, the National Security Council, the President and the Administration spent *14 month planning the war in Iraq even after we had* won in Afghanistan.

The Pentagon is always planning for possible problems around the world. They discuss *every* possibility. al Qaeda, bin Ladin and Saddam, Iraq and Afghanistan all were *carefully studied by many administrations* and *many options were looked over! It is their job!* Be Prepared!! But, some liberals and the *media keep making it a federal case* that the President **wanted to go to war**.........as you can see, very unfounded and absolutely no proof of any kind.....just *innuendo!!!!* **Win the next election!!**

In a reported interview with General Tommy Franks, the retired leader of U.S. troops in Iraq and Afghanistan, he said that President Bush was in no hurry to get into war with Iraq. He said Bush was always a good leader, calm, studious and deliberative and was never steamrolled by his top advisors. He was always his own man.

Most soldiers he said, would agree with "*get the job done*". General Franks also said that the President did his job with *honesty and integrity* and that the mainstream press *got it all wrong*. He also mentioned that no administration would have gone on, *as usual,* after 9-11, and that we were far better off without Saddam.

While President, *Clinton* was faced with the first World Trade Center bombing, the bombing in Saudi Arabia that killed five U. S. military, the Khobar Towers bombing in Saudi Arabia which killed 19 and injured 200 U. S. military, the bombing of the U.S. embassies in Africa which killed 224 and injured 5,000, the bombing of the U.S.S. Cole which killed 17 and injured 39 U.S. sailors.

After each of these events Clinton promised to hunt down and punish those responsible. It never happened and we now wonder if he had kept his promise, would it have prevented the 9-11 attacks. Interestingly*, the Clinton administration pursued with* vigor, over that period of time, *chasing down* Bill Gates at Microsoft.

What are YOU going to do about it?

=============

ACTUAL WORD--FOR WORD—IN COURT!!

Attorney: How old is your son, the one Living with you?

Witness: Thirty-eight or thirty-five, I can't remember!

Attorney: How long has he lived with you?

Witness: FORTY-FIVE YEARS!!!!

===============

A Twelve Year Search and Investigation!

U.S. CASUALTIES IN IRAQ:

*T*his is the most cynical. Way out of perspective! Where are U.S. military the safest? Look at these statistics:

Average of near *2 U.S. military killed daily in Iraq* over 4 years. (Less than 3,000 in combat thru the middle of 2007).

Keeping that figure of 2, in mind, consider that an average of *8 are killed DAILY* by gunfire just in California alone.

A new statistic just released by the government indicates that 4,700 U.S. citizens *are murdered* every year right *here in America* just by *illegal immigrants*.

Also near *50 are murdered DAILY in the U. S.* (at least one and near two a day or more in every major city and 4 are murdered *DAILY just by kids*). Over 18,000 total annually!!! 30 killed in Chicago schools in 07–08.

We now find that reportedly Washington D.C. has a higher murder ratio per capita than Iraq. Yes, they are

---

What are YOU going to do about it?

safer in Iraq than in Washington, D.C. (or perhaps New Orleans too). Hard to believe, but more military lost their lives in peacetime 1980 than during the height of the insurgency in 2006. Now do you understand that the military deaths in Iraq are very miniscule?

Virginia Tech: 33 students/teachers *killed in one day*! How much of those statistics make our front-pages when comparing the deaths in Iraq?

Do you realize that 28 people were killed in Milwaukee just *over a Memorial Day* weekend?
Six citizens were *killed on a weekend* in New Orleans and another *nine in a ten-day period*.

10,000 (that's 10 thousand not 2) were killed on D-Day alone (one day), and a total of *400,000 in WWII!*

36 Million Germans and Japanese were killed during WWII as we nearly destroyed their countries!!!
And look at this: 8,000 Wisconsin boys were lost in WWII - *less than 80 in Iraq*!

Tragically at one point in WWII, up to 3,000 Russian soldiers were killed daily. *DAILY!!*

Listening to the current liberal media (near 100 % in most areas of the nation), or Democrats, sounds like Iraq is like WW II. *Every local or even statewide Iraq death* gets a weeks local TV reporting with many interviews of grieving family and friends, funerals, etc. Some TV segments last up to 4 minutes or 25% of their actual news time. *This is repeated several times daily* for a week! Some stations even show a scoreboard with the number of deaths to date. More brainwashing!

If you watch CNN, MSNBC, NBC, CBS, ABC or read any news from the AP or the Gannett papers (all northeastern Wisconsin newspapers including USA Today) you get bombarded with this negative *reporting on a daily basis* (there are few alternatives). Many are now partners with some TV stations. Interesting: media approval ratings has dropped to 28 % from a high of 37% in 2000! And they like to put the Presidents ratings in the news almost daily when his fall, but never print or report their own ratings. More double standard in the nations media!

Has the media told you that: In 2006, 47 countries had re-established embassies in Iraq and that the Iraqi government employs 1.2 million Iraqis' or that

---

What are YOU going to do about it?

3100 schools have been renovated and 364 are being worked on and 263 new schools are being built.

There are *70 Universities and colleges* operating. They have a Navy with near 40 crafts, and 3 operational air force squadrons with near 30 planes and helicopters (all under Iraqi control). There are 5 Police Academies *producing 3,500 officers every 8 weeks.*

In 2007, the administration reported that oil production was increasing, and the Iraq GDP was rising fast. There are (middle of 2007) approximately 135,000 police, 135,000 Army personnel and 137,000 Defense forces that have been trained.

There are also *1100 new building projects* plus the schools mentioned, plus 67 public clinics, 15 new hospitals, 83 railroad stations, 22 oil facilities, 93 water and 69 electrical facilities.

96% of Iraqi children have received vaccinations and 4.3 million Iraqi children are *enrolled in primary* schools. There are also over 1 million cell phone subscribers, 75 radio stations, 180 newspapers and 10 television stations. (Defense Dept. Web Site)!

ATROCITIES:

Way out of proportion by liberals and the media. Have you or they forgotten *the real atrocities* of Hitler, Japan and North Vietnam. I hope no one has to be reminded! *The concentration camps, the gas chambers, the holocausts in* Poland, Germany and other places that killed millions, the forced marches, prison camps, etc., etc! Unfortunately, most Americans are now at the age where they were not *around for WWII* and do not realize that we really had these problems. *Like it's ancient history and not relevant!*

Real atrocities include pulling out finger nails and cutting off finger, ears or hands, etc., pushing people off buildings, no food for days or weeks, no waste removal, no heat, sleeping on cement and unbearable beatings, hanging people by their thumbs for hours or upside down for hours, stretching racks, etc. Those are real tortures, not taking a few pictures of terrorists in the nude. *But many do-gooders listen* to the radical liberals and accuse us of atrocities. SAD!!! *Just to make a point for re-election in the future!*

What are YOU going to do about it?

What's far worse?......remember the female senior high school students in Illinois a few years ago who *hazed, beat and forced freshmen to eat feces*! (Sending many to the hospital including some with broken bones)! Or how about frat hazing that has **KILLED DOZENS of college students**? *All far worse* than a few humiliating nude pictures of terrorists, sleep depravation, shackles, scare tactics with dogs or lengthy interrogations, many of which are commonly used in our prisons and jails! (Nothing that caused any deaths)!

It is vitally necessary to get quick information out of terrorists in order to save military or general public lives. Obviously some of the alleged tactics in Iraq were not quite politically proper and the necessary legal action has sent some of those responsible to prison. It was very isolated and performed by a few idiots according *to many investigations by Congress* and the Military. It has been **proven** that *it was not, as continually insinuated by the press and liberals, orders from the administration! More brainwashing!*

WAR ON TERROR:

We must always remember who the terrorists are and what they stand for! All branches of these Muslim extremists, al Qaeda, Hamas, Hazbollah or one of the other many groups are all virtually the same. These terrorists have been operating for nearly three decades or more. Their one aim is to *destroy all Western civilization* including the U.S. and Israel, no matter how, *(frequently* their leaders have publicly said this). Some of their tactics included recruiting *12 year olds* with a TV cartoon to become *suicide bombers*. Saddam and Iran sent huge money payments to families of those who blew themselves up as suicide bombers in Israel. One suicide bomber was a young woman and a child in a baby buggy! A recent poll shows that 1 of 4 U.S. *Muslims are OK* with suicide bombers. Which would lead many to believe that it could start here anytime!

Besides sending numerous suicide bombers including teens and women into Israel killing hundreds of innocent people in pizza parlors, malls, etc., they also were responsible for killing 241 of our Marines in the bombing in Biruit in 1983. They also blew-up several airliners killing hundreds. A cruise ship was taken over by these terrorists and killed a handicap man in a wheel chair throwing him over board and then kidnapped and killed many Israel athletes at the Olympics plus the train bombings in Madrid and London.

It began in 1979 when Iran radicals, with the blessing of their religious leaders, took over and held our embassy hostage for hundreds of days with Carter as President. Other U.S. Embassies were bombed around the world and the USS Cole was targeted killing many U.S. Sailors. al Qaeda and bin Ladin also were responsible for the first bombing of the World Trade Center in 1993 and then the recent killing of 3,000 in the World Trade Center destruction on 9-11.

In 1998, bin Laden announced to the world "*it was in the Muslim religion to hate and kill anyone not of his faith*". He blamed the poor Muslim economy and the poor conditions of their countries on the U.S. and Israel even though the U.S. had, for many years, given billions of dollars in aid to many of these countries and *some Muslim/Arab countries were extremely rich.* No one will ever know how this money was used.

Can anyone find a sensible reason, any reason, to support those who are involved in these horrendous activities throughout the world without any regard to innocent citizens of any country?

It is unbelievable that a Carter era judge, a highly liberal female, who gave money donations to the ACLU, gave the radical ACLU their wishes and banned the U.S. method of tracking down terrorists through listening to terrorists phone calls, the internet, etc. A great and hard working tool for catching these horrendous terrorists! *Once again,* a liberal judge, without regard to the nations safety, tried to embarrass the President in an effort to bring about change in the election. NO MATTER THE CONSEQUENCES!

Recently, an al Qaeda terrorist camp, *"graduated"* several hundred volunteer suicide bombers and sent them world wide. *Any problem here?*

Many factors are siding with the terrorists or those supporting terrorists. In 2006, the best foreign film in the Golden Globe Awards honored terrorists who were suicide bombers in Palestine and seemed to claim that it is a legitimate tactic against Israel and Iraq and many other countries around the world.

Perhaps we need another General, Chief-of-staff, like General Black Jack Pershing. A General since 1906, he was Military Governor of the Moro Province in the Philippines in 1909 and General of the Armies in1919 and Chief of Staff in 1921.

It is told, that just before WWI, there was a number of terrorists attacks on U.S. forces in the Philippines by Muslim Extremists. The General captured 50 of them and tied them to posts for execution (permitted then). He then brought in two pigs and had them slaughtered in front of the horrified terrorists. Muslims detest pork and refuse to eat or even touch. To do so, bars them from paradise (and their virgins) and doomed to hell.

The soldiers then soaked their bullets in pigs blood and executed *49* of them. The soldiers dug a hole, buried them only after dumping the pigs blood and entails, etc., on top of them. They let the *50'th man* watch and then let him go and for the next 45 years there was not a single Muslim attack anywhere in the world. Maybe it's time to find another Black Jack Pershing to go to Iran, Syria or Lebanon. Pork anyone?

Rick Mathes, a well known leader in prison ministry, had to attend a seminar to continue his prison ministry. He reported that part of it was a presentation by a Catholic, a Protestant and a Muslim explaining their faiths and what they believed in.

After listening to the Islamic Imam, Mathes asked, *"Please correct me if I'm wrong, but I understand that most Imams and clerics of Islam, have declared a holy jihad against the infidels of the world. And, that by killing an infidel, which is a command to all Muslims, they are assured of a place in heaven. If that is the case, can you give me the definition of an infidel"? Without hesitation, he replied, "non-believers"!*

Mathes responded, "So, let me make sure I have this straight. All followers of Allah have been commanded to kill everyone who is not of your faith so they can go to heaven. Is that correct"? He sheepishly replied, "Yes"!

Mathes then stated, "Well sir, I have a real problem trying to imagine the Pope or a Protestant leader, commanding all Catholics or Christians to kill those of your faith in order to get to heaven"! The Imam was speechless! Mathes continued, "I also have a problem with being your friend when you and your brother clerics are telling followers to kill me! Would you rather have your Allah who tells you to kill me in order to go to heaven, or my Jesus who tells me to love you because I am going to heaven and he wants you to be with me"? You could hear a pin drop as the IMAM HUNG HIS HEAD IN SHAME!!!!

Clearly, *not all Muslims* are called to kill all infidels, but I challenge those who are not, to speak up and denounce those who are.

The article above by Rick Mathes, (www.missiongateministry.org), was written to the *radical Muslims who consider America the Great* Satan. Our thanks to Rick for giving us permission to print.

Remember, *"that the truth will prevail"!!*

Let's take a look at Iran. One of the Worlds worst terrorist states. And if you do not believe that Iran is a threat to the whole of Western Civilization and will go to any length to destroy all of us, take a look at THIS INFORMATION from the defense Department web site. It is very scary!!

Iran has dozens of long range missal sites, chemical weapons sites, early warning sites, sites working on or building nuclear weapons, biohazard missal sites, mobile scud missal sites, silk worm sites, etc., etc. Up and down their coasts and borders with Iraq, Saudi Arabia, Kuwait, Turkey, Pakistan.

You might be interested to know that Iran's economy is in shambles because of the suppressive regime and the economic sanctions imposed by most of the rest of the world. It is relatively sad, because they are perfectly capable of holding their own on the worlds financial stage as they have the second largest supply of natural gas, 15%, and 10% of the worlds oil reserves. They also have a supply of low grade Uranium.

Unfortunately they have high illiteracy, high birthrates and have long been involved in many bloody wars and revolutions. Unemployment is round 15%.

An Immigrant from Croatia back many years ago wrote the following "Letter-to-the-Editor" but it was refused in a California newspaper:

"Dear Editor,   (Paraphrased for shortness)!
...those arriving at Ellis Island by ship had to stand in long lines and said good-bye to their birth place to give their children a new life. Nothing was handed to them. No free lunches, no welfare, no labor laws to protect them. All they had was the skills and craftsmanship they brought with them.

Most of the children of these immigrants came of age when WWII started. My father fought along side men whose parents had come straight over from Germany, Italy, France, Ireland and Japan.

None of these 1'st generation Americans ever gave any thought about what country their parents had come from. They were Americans fighting Hitler, Mussolini and the Emperor of Japan. They were defending the U.S. of America as one people. No one in France looked at these liberators as French-Americans or German-Americans or Irish-Americans. They were Americans carrying one flag. They had stirred the melting pot into one red, white and blue bowl.

Now, in 2006-07, a new kind of immigrant wants the same rights and privileges. Only they want to achieve it by playing with a different set of rules. Ones that includes an entitlement card and a guarantee of being faithful to their mother country. I'm sorry, that's not what being an American is all about. These original immigrants would be appalled that they are being used as an example by those waving foreign flags. They deserve better than that for the toil, hard work and sacrifice in raising these future generations to create a land that has become a beacon for those legally searching for a better life".
(Signed)

A Twelve Year Search and Investigation!

DEFENSE SPENDING:

Another myth perpetuated by the liberal left, insists that we are spending too much on defense, which could be used for other things. The fact is that the average percentage of the national budget spent on Defense and the percentage of GDP spent on Defense *has dropped annually for the last few decades*. In '07 the war costs are down to 1% of the $63 Trillion GDP. Miniscule. U. S. GDP has increased 16% during war.

Under Eisenhower, 53% of budget for defense and 10% of GDP. Under Johnson, 45% of budget and 9% of GDP. Under Reagan 26% of budget. In 2006 *under President Bush, 19% of budget and 3.8% of GDP and now in 2007, only 1%!* (From the Washington Times). Meanwhile, spending for other government social programs increased dramatically!

We continually hear that we do not take care of our veterans when returning from action. It's interesting to know that just here in Wisconsin, the Veterans Administration now has three huge hospitals and have opened 15 clinics around the State. Most of these new clinics have come about since the end of

What are YOU going to do about it?

the Vietnam and Korean Wars. Many built under the Bush Administration within the last few years, including a big, efficient and professional one in Appleton and new clinics in La Crosse and Green Bay.

Nationwide the VA operates 155 Hospitals, 135 Nursing Homes, 45 Residential Rehabilitation Treatment programs, 155 Hospital based Outpatient Clinics, 721 Outpatient Clinics, 5 mobile Clinics and 207 Veterans Centers. *Near 1,400 facilities.*

Thousands of Veterans are now able to get professional treatment close to home rather that having to travel previously to the only two, Milwaukee and Tomah, here in Wisconsin. (Most of this information very under-reported by the liberal media). Nationwide the VA treats near 5.5 million veterans with near 1 million visits weekly.

Recently, the liberals and the media got another gift from the press. A newspaper investigative report revealed that a *temporary* holding facility, for *ambulatory* veterans, *across the street* from the Walter Reed Hospital, (an old hotel *scheduled for demolition),* had some apparent unsanitary conditions. (Why not just reveal to the Pentagon so that it could be fixed rather than making it a national disaster story bashing the President who personally had nothing to do with the problem, other than being President. *Could there be liberal bias there)? A very isolated problem*, but the liberal press and democrats in Congress were quick to pile it on contending that the *whole VA* and *all military hospitals* and the *whole DOD* system and *of course the President* was negligent and knowingly (how ridiculous) putting the returning veterans in jeopardy and poor health situations. *The usual liberal spin!*

But I have yet to see a liberal station or press report that a new VA $50 million rehab hospital had just opened. Or how all the new VA clinics are really great. Not a peep! After our local paper reported the problems at Walter Reed (which is not a VA hospital), there were many letters to the editor, telling how great the local VA clinic was.

What are YOU going to do about it?

WE KILL NEARLY 100 PEOPLE

EVERY DAY IN THE U.S.!

50 ARE MURDERED AND

OVER 40 KILLED BY DRUNKS!

HOW MANY U.S. MILITARY
ARE KILLED DAILY IN IRAQ ???

2

A LITTLE PERSPECTIVE!

Please !

A Twelve Year Search and Investigation!

CHAPTER VI

MORAL BREAKDOWN!

*T*he liberal, secular Hollywood, liberal, secular judges, ACLU, liberal democrats in Congress, secular college professors, NAACP leadership and the NEA unions are increasingly leading us down the *road of moral decay* similar to most European countries where *Christianity has nearly disappeared.* Statistics show that church memberships in the U. S. are declining and more and more anti-Christian sentiments are becoming the norm in liberal University teachings, public schools, rulings from liberal benches and congressional discussions!

Radical atheists are heavily involved in bringing anti-Christian law change into our court systems and *finding liberal sympathic judges* in some instances.

Example of moral breakdown: near 1 million abortions every year (teens responsible for 19%) and now anyone can purchase the day after abortion pill without prescription---one more nail in the moral breakdown casket. How many abortions with this pill?

What are YOU going to do about it?

Many schools now pass out condoms and give advice on abortion. It's becoming the norm like sex, violence, language and drug use that we see every day in movies and TV and from questioning our young students and adults!

(For a more complete look at what the NEA is doing nationwide with sex education, please refer to "**The Enemy Within", by Michael Savage.** Eye opening)!!!

It is now estimated that nearly 2,200 children go missing *each and every day* on average and there are also an estimated 300,000 sex offenders in the U.S.

In 2007, a high school in Boulder Colorado brought in an evidently liberal, anti-Christian panel to discuss sex and drugs. Reportedly, they told the students assembled, that they should experiment with various drugs and sex including same sex partners. The school administration had refused requests by students and parents to have a second opinion for a fair and balanced presentation. *Do we have a Moral Breakdown? PROVEN!!!* And this same panel was invited back for 2008!

Recently, a junior high school took students on a field trip to a Family Planning clinic. Can you imagine!!! Also recently, a school board ruled that a football coach could not say a prayer with his team at the beginning of a game. Or how about a high school band given notice that they could not play "Ave Maria", music version, no words, at a band concert.

And now, newly reported, a school system in Maine is discussing allowing 11 to 14 year olds (middle school children), permission to get birth control pills from the school nurse without parental notice. They have been giving condoms out since 2000.

Know we hear of a state bar association, banning a proposed lawyer from joining the bar, because he was against gay marriage! (Legal action is ongoing)! AND WE DON'T HAVE A PROBLEM? How about the 9'th Circuit Court (California obviously) ruling that rape is <u>not</u> a serious offense and didn't result in jail time.

What does this lead to? Nearly 3,000 divorces *daily* and over 5 million Americans are cohabiting compared to ½ million in 1970 and 60% of all marriages are preceded by cohabitation. Marriage preceded by cohabitation is *46% more likely* to end in

---

What are YOU going to do about it?

divorce. Now we find that intimate partner violence affects 32 million in the U.S. DO WE HAVE A PROBLEM?? Studies now show that divorces and single parent families, cost the U.S. $112 Billion annually---*as costly as the Iraq war.*

1 in 4 children are exposed to alcoholism in their homes? Then we find that approximately 1 in 6 teens have gone to school drunk. In the Philadelphia school system, there were 500 assaults on teachers during the school year '06-'07. There are now an estimated 130,000 **teens in PRISON!** Plus 8 out of 10 will be *back in jail after a year of freedom* after serving time.

A few years ago just in Baltimore alone, 80,000 were reportedly addicted to heroin or cocaine. New studies show that *60 million* (20%) in the U.S. are addicted to drugs, porn, gambling or alcohol. Some studies show that near 80% of those who use marijuana leads to heroin or cocaine. Many liberals continue to tell us that using marijuana is not harmful. Again, numerous medical studies have proven that marijuana is very harmful to our bodies and our minds with regular use.

Nationwide, $14 million is lost daily through gambling. In Wisconsin alone we now have somewhere near 250,000 addicted to gambling. Imagine, nearly a quarter of a million of our neighbors here in America's heartland. *Is this a problem?* Losing homes, divorces **AND SEVERE FAMILY DISCORD,** job losses, BANKRUPTCIES, etc. How great is that???

Nationally $9 **billion** is spent on pornography and $15 **billion** spent on prostitution. **1/3 of all girls** under 13 have had intercourse. There is a home break-in every 15 seconds or *5,760 daily!* Do we have a moral breakdown in the U. S.? Not really a question!!!

How about the 15,000 killed on our highways by drunk drivers every year at *a cost of over $45 billion*! Especially here in Wisconsin we have a society that more and more looks the other way at our addiction to alcohol. Now we discover that **41% of 9'th graders** drink regularly. 1 in 5 auto deaths are drug related.

Marriage reduces poverty. Poverty rate of children in single families is 38%. Only 8.1% in married families. Tax payers spend $500 billion each year on Food Stamps, Medicaid and needy family assistance. Married men less likely to commit crime and marriage increases taxable income earnings over $61 billion. Reducing family fragmentation by only 1% leads to

---

What are YOU going to do about it?

$1.12 billion in taxpayer savings. Above statistics by The Heritage Foundation.

In 2006 the city of Milwaukee lead the nation in alcohol consumption. The University of Wisconsin has lead Universities for the same reason frequently.

Go to any Professional NFL, NBA or NHL game and you can see many fans over-indulging, sitting in the stands with children all around them like idiots.

At many business meetings, church functions, sports events, family gatherings, we frequently see the use of alcohol as one of the main social staples. And many will over-indulge **even with children** in attendance. Are we setting a good example? *Not so!*

Many of our high school teens are arrested for underage drinking and when entering college have a *tendency to become binge drinkers* in their freshman year. Another recent study showed that nearly 3,200 teens died last year *just from alcohol poisoning.* Thousands of teens also die from alcohol related accidents or disease each and every year.

Wisconsin is #1 in drunk drivers! *Roll models?* SURE!

ARCHAIC U.S. SENATE

After watching the U.S. Senate in session on C-Span for the last several years, it has become very obvious that our tax money is being wasted by the archaic methods used in the management and operation of the Senate.

Much of the time, in fact, most of the time, when a Senator is on the Senate floor, giving testimony on a resolution being debated, presenting an amendment, introducing a new resolution, etc., he is the only one in the Senate Chamber (except for the permanent employees at desk jobs). There may be one other in the Chamber, usually the Senator who is next in line to have the floor to speak and is waiting for his turn. When the Senator is finished he usually leaves the floor and goes to his office or lunch or meetings. No other Senator hears his colleagues' frame of mind or his testimony. Useless except for a few hundred watching c-span.

Most Senate hearings are at best slightly better. Senate committees will frequently request or demand that supposed experts testify on the subject of the meeting. All well and good! But, frequently, *the only Senator showing up* at the start of the meeting is the chairman and maybe one or two others and then during the testimony of these experts, having assembled materials and taking time to appear, *a few senators may show up and many leave* after asking their questions. The committee usually consists of a dozen or more but seldom is there more than a few at the meeting. Yet there is seating for a couple dozen Senators and those *testifying are frequently talking to empty chairs.*

During these committee hearings, many Senators are conversing with aids, walking in and out of the room, discussing things with other Senators, all the while testimony *of experts is going on.* Being exceptionally rude is not the worst part of this situation. Not listening to these experts and not knowing what is said *is the worst.* Why call these people and then not listen.

Recently, the Treasurer of the United States was testifying before a Senate Committee. The two ranking chairmen held a conference at the podium *while the official was giving testimony* directly in front of him. *Beyond rude!!* Only two others present!

Senators are usually given two 5 or 10 minute periods to ask questions of the experts who have been requested or required to appear at a Senate Committee hearing and do much preparing testimony for these hearings. Rudeness by liberal Democrats is the theme of the day. Many will go on for 4 & 1/2 minutes ranting with liberal rhetoric and then ask a question in their last ½ minute allowed.

Many times they rudely *demand* a yes or no answer and not getting it they rant and rave that the person is not being forthcoming or explain they have run out of time and cut short the person presenting the testimony, interrupting and constantly grilling with no chance for the person to answer. This practice is common in many hearings. When the Senator finishes his grilling, he will usually leave the hearing room and not listen to any other testimony. Beyond rude!!

Frequently on the Senate floor, a quorum is called. Which means *that nothing is going on* in the Chamber. These quorums may go on for a short time or can last hours while leaders are determining what to do next, or waiting for someone to come to the floor or negotiations are going on between parties.

What are YOU going to do about it?

Meanwhile, *20 or more employees and pages* having desk jobs in the Chamber, are sitting with nothing to do.

Many evenings and mornings, when the Senate is not in official session, Senators are given time to make speeches. C-Span will televise these speeches, which **have turned into political rhetoric for hours at a time.** Frequently, liberal Senators will have the floor and turn it into a dramatic show with several members discussing a perceived problem created by the Conservatives or the Administration or just plain bashing the President.

Voting in the Senate is the most archaic. When a vote is called for, many times few Senators are on the floor. They call it a fifteen-minute vote. Seldom is a vote less than a ½ hour and many times it will proceed for over an hour or even longer on occasion. Each *member must come to the podium* and by voice or body action, indicate how they are voting AND THEY HAVE TO BE RECOGNIZED BY THE VOTING RECORDER.

They are probably one of the few government entities anywhere that does not use electronic voting. We all see this on our local televisions. City councils, county boards, state legislators, etc., all are usually in the meeting room at all times, *listening to testimony* of outsiders or their own members on legislation. They *then punch a button on their desks to vote.* Takes less than a minute. They are familiar with everything and know how their fellow members think or they have the *testimony from special experts.*

So much for being practical and efficient! Committee meetings are not an excuse. Most all county boards, local city councils, state legislatures, etc., all have committee meetings and hearings but most have electronic voting methods when meeting in the whole.

A WEE BIT PERSPECTIVE!

WE LOST 10,000
 IN A SINGLE DAY
  (ONE DAY)!!!
   IN WWII ! (D-DAY)

WE LOST LESS THAN
 3,000 IN 4 YEARS
  IN IRAQ !

FRIENDS OF THE HELPLESS!!!

Another very serious bias in the media and with liberal democrats has to do with which party has better helped the poor, race relations, voting biases, etc., over the years. The liberals always have said they are the party of the poor, minorities and women. Unfortunately it is frequently given legs by the liberal media. *This is a major myth!*

Conservative Republicans have a long history of civil rights. The party was formed in 1854 to address the issue of slavery and also addressed racism as a moral issue in its first platform in 1856.

Republicans single handedly passed the 14th and 15th Amendments to the Constitution to guarantee the rights of citizenship and voting for all Americans, with *not one Democrat* in Congress voting for either and in its first 14 years of controlling Congress, Republicans passed 23 civil rights laws, each over almost unanimous opposition by Democrats.

The 1964 Civil Rights Act and the 1965 Voting Rights Act were passed because of strong Republican support and the Republican Party has a proud record of standing up for moral issues and for the inalienable rights of every individual.

The Republican Party has a history and moral commitment against racism and continues to *welcome Americans of every ethnicity* to take seats at the table in their party as they work together to preserve our heritage, religious freedom, strong family values and ethical morals and it still carries on that tradition.

(From the www.wisgop.org web site)

ILLEGAL IMMIGRATION:

*P*resident Theodore Roosevelt in 1907 said:

"In the first place, we should insist that if the immigrant who comes here in good faith, becomes an American and assimilates himself to us, he shall be treated on an exact equality with everyone else, for it is an outrage to discriminate against any such man because of creed, birthplace or origin. BUT, this is predicated upon the person's becoming in every facet an American and nothing but an American...There can be no divided allegiance here. Any man who says he is an American, but something else also, isn't an American at all. We have room for but one flag...We have room for just one language here, and that is the English language...and we have room for but one sole loyalty and that is a loyalty to the American people."

Increasingly, illegal immigration is becoming a very serious problem in many states. California, Florida, Texas, Arizona, L.A., Michigan and New York appear to have the worst problems, but it appears to be evident throughout the entire country to some degree even here in the Midwest.

What are YOU going to do about it?

In L.A. county, it has been reported by the *Los Angeles Times*, that, out of near 10.2 million residents, *near 40% are working for cash* and pay no taxes and close to 95% of warrants for murder and *75% of all those wanted for crimes,* are illegal immigrants. Even in the nearly white population of most of the Midwest, we frequently see Asian or African Americans being arrested, identified and/or convicted of various crimes. Reported nearly nightly on TV news.

Recently a liberal, Clinton appointed, federal judge, ruled that a prison program, Bible based, funded by private donations and completely voluntary by prisoners, was illegal because it "promotes Christianity"! However, at the same time, taxpayers are forced to pay for special Muslim Koran Bibles, prayer rugs, and special facilities for worship for those of the Muslim faith.

One more step in the secular direction being forced on America by the radical ACLU and anti-Christian judges who have created, out of thin air, the separation of church and state. There is *no mention* of this rule or law in any of our original federal documents. The only close section *forbids any government entity from starting a religion* and **requires** the government not to stop any religion from operating. *"SEPARATION OF CHURCH AND STATE"* does not exist! It is *a fabrication* of the ACLU!

Near 60% of all HUD properties are in illegal hands and according to a Rice University study, the cost estimate of illegal immigrants to the American tax payer, after subtracting any taxes paid by immigrants, was a net $70 BILLION way back in 1997. It may be safe to say that this figure has at least doubled by 2006. Some studies show $68 Billion is the annual cost.

Interestingly, nearly 30% of those serving time in federal prisons are illegal immigrants. Just in Orange County only, in California, there are approximately 275 gangs with 17,000 members, 98% of which are Mexican or Asian and the Wall Street Journal reported that Asian mobsters are the "*greatest criminal challenge in the country*". (FBI statistics)!! It has also been reported that in L.A. County there is one gang with near 20,000 members, 40% of which are illegal immigrants.

What are YOU going to do about it?

Can you imagine the terrible problems confronting teachers, social workers, health facilities, health personnel, law enforcement, etc.? Hundreds of people in L.A. are killed or maimed by gangs annually.

Fortunately, the present administration has started making efforts to curb this tragic problem that has been neglected for several decades. President Bush and the 2006 Republican Congress authorized the building of a 700 mile fence with $1.2 billion starting funds, they have doubled the number of border enforcement officers, brought in the National Guard for back-up in some spots and increased funding and equipment aids for the border patrol. Early results show a big improvement to date in 2007.

Government enforcement agencies are also examining businesses who may be employing illegals in violation of existing laws. Corporate executives have been arrested and fined and many illegals, having fake credentials, bought on the black market, from thieves stealing personal identities, have been deported or put into prison. Several States and even some cities and counties have also begun enforcement efforts. We found that 1 in 3 immigrants were illegals.

Whether or not the fence will be worthwhile depends on the method and *type of fence.* Some liberals have made efforts to stop this fence by saying it will not work or its too expensive.

What will work: A double fence similar to maximum prison security fences with 15 feet or so between fences filled with barbed wire rolls and 15 feet tall with razor wire at the top and built into at least 6 feet of concrete underground and with electrical charge and electronic/video motion sensors alerting a central observation post with capabilities of responding within minutes. (Not just a 10-foot wall that is easy to scale or dig under). It will cost, but look at the cost of having illegals here in the States, at near $150 Billion annually. It will be *very* cost effective in the long run.

Some liberals fight these efforts saying we shouldn't put up a fence like the Berlin Wall for public relations reasons. Apples and oranges! The Berlin Wall was built by the Communists to keep people from escaping into the free world to West Berlin. The wall between Mexico and the U. S. *will keep out illegal immigrant drug carriers, hardened criminals, perhaps even terrorists, etc.,* from entering illegally. Unfortunately, many are coming just to work and we

What are YOU going to do about it?

should have compassion for them. But, they must come legally!

It is estimated that near 30% of the estimated 400,000 crossing the border, are drug traffickers and/or hardened criminals of all types (nearly 120,000 annually). *Unfortunately, many ignore this part of the immigration problem* and just try to protect the unfortunate souls looking for job opportunities and many of us just trying to be nice to minorities. The liberals like to be "politically correct" no matter the consequences! *Perhaps future voters?*

Interestingly, it is estimated that in 1992, there were near 160,000 illegal immigrant children attending schools in Arizona. What's your guess now, 9 years later? In Florida, one county in 2007 had 338 illegals in their jail at an average annual cost of $40,000 per prisoner.

By the year 2050, 25% of the U.S. population will be Hispanic. Jumping from near 42 million now, to near *100 million.* In a Catholic Church in Falls Church, Virginia, the pastor has stated that 70% of Baptisms are in Spanish, yet only 35% of his parish is Hispanic. But there are other very real problems: There is a very high rate of Hispanic high school dropouts, a large number are on welfare and research shows that parents want their children to retain fluency in Spanish.

40% lack a high school education compared to 16% of the general population and the median income in the Hispanic households is nearly $13,000 less than white households. Do you realize that studies show that only 2% of illegals are working picking crops, but 41% are on welfare. Or that 43% of food stamps and 41% of unemployment checks go to illegals. No problem there?

If you go to ImmigrationCounters.com, you'll find estimated real-time data on illegal immigration statistics that show the huge problem that this has become. For your information we publish the June 7, 2007 stats. Our thanks to ImmigrationCounters.com!

20,933,888 – Number of Illegal Immigrants

$31,657,423,744 – Money wired to Mexico since January of 2006

What are YOU going to do about it?

$273,941,682,897 – Money wired to Latin America since 2001

$397,460,018,501 – Cost of Social Services to Illegals since 1996

4,028,223 – Children of Illegals in Public Schools

$14,230,175,927 – Cost of illegals in K–12 since 1996

338,275 – Numbers of Illegals in Jails or Prisons

$1,422,429,407 – Cost of those illegals incarcerated.

649,111 – Illegal immigrant wanted fugitives.

9,983,302 – Skilled jobs taken by Illegal Immigrants.

A Twelve Year Search and Investigation!

CHAPTER VII

ECONOMY AND JOBS

There are many economists and investment experts saying that the current economic expansion is stronger than during the Clinton years. Preposterous, of course, (according to liberal Democrats). But look at the statistics! **Clinton faced no** challenges as he inherited an excellent Republican economy growing at the rate of more than 4%. ***It soared until it collapsed*** in 2000 when the stocks clipped $8 Trillion in wealth. **Joblessness boomed.** The *economy was shrinking!* But we had a surplus??...(Only on paper)!

President Bush faced this recession left by the Clinton era and then faced 9-11. Both gave us *massive* hits on the economy (***then throw in Katrina*** which damaged many oil rigs in the Gulf and damaged refineries on the coast). But the administrations tax cuts brought it slowly back 'till we now have an even greater economy (even with Iraq).

Unemployment down to 4.4% (under 4% in many places) in early 2007 and real after tax incomes have risen $2,900 per person since the President took office. The stock market is breaking records nearly daily (50% of Americans depend to some extent on a good market) and near 10 million new jobs created since 2001 and on top of that, *productivity grew* at 2.8% a year outstripping the average for the last three decades.

Which means that Americans have amassed more wealth, bigger incomes, larger homes (MORE OWNING HOMES THAN EVER) better health (great new Medicare and drug programs for seniors), and are better educated than ever (people with a degree has increased from 8% to near 30%, in just a few decades).

Unfortunately, *liberals driven by petty vengeance*, seem to want to ruin everything by raising taxes, ignoring reforms that are crucial in Social Security and Medicare and they enjoy punishing those who have been successful by piling on taxes, which is called (COMMUNISM)! Higher taxation for business means higher prices for the consumer. Very simple!

Recent budget resolutions proposed by the *Democrats could raise taxes by $2,641* per household, if enacted, each year, over the next

A Twelve Year Search and Investigation!

decade and kill 709,000 jobs and $200 Billion in personal income according to tax analyst Brian Reidl of the Heritage Foundation. All because of their *hatred of the President!!!* Do they care for people?

As a said earlier, a Republican Congress in the Clinton years, and Clinton inheriting a great economy, were the reasons for a great economy in the 90's. Nothing Clinton did! Yet he got all the media credit. But yet there is still, even today, unfounded, *media driven, economic anxiety* and absolutely *no credit to anyone* for the current boom. Mostly because we hear erroneous story after story in the national media and from liberal politicians about how bad the economy is. REALLY!!! *Their scare tactic rhetoric with absolutely no reason* may end the boom. How sad!

Interestingly, Europe in 2006 had skyrocketing, double-digit unemployment, double-digit inflation and gas prices approaching $10.00 per gallon. Their economy a disaster! Statistically WE HAVE THE GREATEST ECONOMY IN THE WORLD! How often has the major media given out that information? AND THE LIBERAL DEMOCRATS and media CONTINUE TO BASH THE ECONOMY!!!! Go figure!

Sure, jobs have gone overseas, **ALWAYS HAVE,** *but many more* millions, near 10 million, have been created *here in the U. S.* from 2001 to 2007. Compared to only 360,000 in Japan and 1.1 million in European countries. We are part of a new global market! Many foreign cars are now made in the U. S. and foreign car companies have *announced* they will be building even more factories in the next few years. *They now have 16 factories here,* providing thousands of new good paying jobs. Honda has announced they will be building a *new U.S. headquarters* in North America. (Has the media informed you of that)? Many financial institutions from overseas have opened facilities and employ thousands. One could go on and on. *20% of U. S. business firms can't find* enough skilled or trained labor.

Buy American...not easy. EXAMPLE: Some Chev's are made in Mexico and other U.S. car companies are planning to move more out of the U.S. because of union demands and to stay competitive, while many Toyota and Honda cars are made in the U.S.

Most all major U.S. companies have factories overseas. Example: Kimberly Clark (Kleenex, etc) has factories in over 50 foreign countries. All we continue to hear, over and over, from liberals, the press and democrat congressmen, is jobs are going to India (which for the most part are poor paying jobs). Just more attempts at brainwashing the public into thinking that our economy is bad!

How wrong can they be when *it is obvious we have the greatest economy in the world.* The chronic poor and minorities believe the liberal fabrication. *We have full employment!* Any warm body that wants a job and *can qualify*, has a job!!! But they *still have to perform* or lose the job and they have to fit into their new environment without bitterness or complaining. (See below).

Or, how about the additional *3 million new jobs* that are expected to be created by high tech companies in the next few years. *Are we training* our kids right? Look to the future, not complain about the past. Lots of programs are out there to help train those who are laid off -- if-- *if they have the ability and desire.*

Locally every time we hear of some company laying off workers or going out of business (always on the front page), the next day we hear of a company hiring another 50, 100 or 200 workers (and one health

---

What are YOU going to do about it?

company announced they will be hiring nearly a thousand new people) or a new business starting up (usually buried on the inside pages).

Remember, it is normal for 4 out 5 new businesses to go out of business within 5 years. That's the way it is and always has been. That's why you see some citizens laid off or small businesses going out, but statistics show they get back into employment very quickly, most within a couple months and you see many vacant buildings being put back to use after a while and new jobs created. There is constant turnover of space and people. The average person in the U. S. has 8 jobs in his or her lifetime. *It's normal!!*

Jobs have increased by the millions in the last 6 years even though the liberals keep shouting from the rooftops that we are sending all our jobs overseas. Talk about ridiculous! MORE BRAINWASHING!!! Wisconsin has seen a growth in manufacturing jobs during the last year and growth is expected into 2008. *Pretty much buried in the local press and TV.*

And yes, the rich get richer....why? Simple!!! Because of the *great economy* over the last 15 years, except for the Clinton recession started in 2000 and ended quickly by the Republicans by 2003. The rich have the resources and the funds necessary to invest in new companies, new equipment, new product lines, bigger advertising budgets, etc., *that create jobs.* These investments (if successful) pay off with new jobs and of course *additional corporate and individual taxes are a huge by-product...YES, because* of the great economy.

Every one is eligible. Get on the bandwagon!! It'*s not tax breaks* for the rich that made them more *money.....every one that paid taxes* received tax breaks (obviously, some would not get any back if they didn't pay any to begin with). (See next paragraph). Statistics show that there are now millions *of new investors* in the stock and bond markets including millions of new seniors. All earning big money as the stock market keeps growing and breaking all time records. Part of the American dream!! Near 160 million U.S. citizens now invest!

NOW HEAR THIS: 2005 showed more tax revenues than ever *in history!!!* And really significant is the fact that *corporate* tax revenues were up 47%! Individuals were up 15%. *So, who got tax breaks?* Obviously, not big business!

What are YOU going to do about it?

Why is it that **most all** national business, investment, economic newspapers are Conservative. Hmmmmm! No wonder we have a great economy!!!

Unbelievable!!! Last year (2006) the *top 1% richest* paid somewhere near *66% of all taxes!!!!* (Can you imagine, top 1%, amazing)! The bottom 40% to 50% *pay little or none!* Seldom does the national media or democrats admit this but always go back to old, tired, favorite talking points that the rich get all the breaks. *These statistics prove otherwise!* What's the saying....oh yaa, ...*more brainwashing!!!*

"The middle class is disappearing", is another favorite talking point myth of the liberals. *Yes, but where are they going?......they are getting richer*! They are moving up into the upper class!! Average real wages and benefits have increased by nearly *40% since 1973* (after adjusting for inflation). Consumers spent an average of over $25,000 **per person** in 2004, nearly **double the amount in 1973.** 8% of those over 25 held a college degree in 1960. *NOW: Near 30%!* (See "Income and Wealth", a new book by Alan Reynolds, a Cato Institute scholar).

Interestingly, the constant plight of the African-American is another favorite liberal ploy. However, new statistics show that in the last three decades, the number of African-Americans who are in the middle class has improved from 1 out of 10, to *1 out of 3.* (No statistics were found showing how many minorities are now in the upper class which has also increased dramatically with every profession, medical, law, business, government, real estate, accounting, education, etc., all with growing minorities).

The plight of low income residents are really miss-represented by the liberals and the press who like to make political statements about the President and the Republicans not taking care of the poor. It has just been reported that those under the poverty line, about 12%, *is very misleading.* New statistics show that the average family under the poverty line is there *only temporarily.* Many are under the line for just a month or two and only about 3% of them last a year or more. Statistics show *that over 90%* of those under the poverty line, *will move up* to the middle class within ten years.

Another myth has to do with the "*distribution of wealth",* which is a real myth. There is no such thing.

What are YOU going to do about it?

Wealth is usually earned not distributed. It is earned through first getting an education. Then, as one works his way through his years after an education, it's how one puts that education to work. Either your own business or working for someone else. Then you are on your way. *Only your own bad decisions, morals,* etc., can stop you from becoming successful.

It also has shown that those under the poverty line spend, on average, *twice as much as their reported income.* They use savings, help from families, government programs, relatives, etc., to get through the relatively short time below the poverty line. Really suffering *are the chronic 3%,* but yet they have many programs, listed below, to help them get through their problems!

Now we find that **college grad hiring in 2007 is up** sharply at nearly 17% with many graduates starting at $40,000 to $55,000 in annual wages. Have you heard that?

We also hear frequently from the liberal left that some 40 million do not have health insurance. When we examined this problem we found the following.... *About 1/3 have the necessary income* to afford

---

A Twelve Year Search and Investigation!

insurance but *fail to purchase. Another 1/3 are eligible for government insurance programs*, but *fail to sign up.* Many in the other 3'rd are millions of illegal aliens. So, the only real problem is *maybe 8 million* (not the 40 million) yet, they may be eligible for other help provided by hospitals, clinics, shelters and drug company programs for the poor. (Insurance Industry Reports). Nothing as usual in the media!

Most of the few chronically unemployed find it impossible to hold or get a job for many reasons. Many are high school drop-outs, *(1.2 million drop out of high school each year), who can't make change, are unable to read, have attitude problems, can't get along with others, have drug problems, are unable to take correction or be trained or take orders from others, have rings sticking out of noses, ears, lips, many (millions) are illegal immigrants, mental problems, millions of ex-cons. Even some graduates have the same problems.*

I've personally seen young females applying for a receptionist position, wearing short shorts and hair not taken care of and some applying who could not fill out an application! *(Nothing caused by the President)!* My wife and I recently went for dinner at a

What are YOU going to do about it?

local supper club. Our female server had rings out of her lips, nose, tongue and ears. My wife nearly threw up and we vowed never to return to that establishment. We notified the manager. But again, it seems like it is becoming common among the young and *many parents accept* this ridiculous practice rather than fight it. The President caused it! RIGHT?

The great economy has resulted in many small retail stores and restaurants, right here in our area, like fast food operations, having to pay $10.00 per hour or more (which is now close to the real minimum wage in the area) and are forced to hire nearly any warm body applying. I think we have all seen the quality of some workers in many places. Fortunately, we have many of these small service businesses that are able to hire these types of workers. Plus we have Wal-Mart and a few others who will hire many unfortunates who cannot get jobs elsewhere like the mentally and physically challenged.

Even though Wal-Mart pays well above the minimum, nearly double, for starting pay, average starting for part-timers about $11.00 per hour, they are continually attacked by liberals for not furnishing health insurance! *Most all retailers* do not furnish insurance or retirement programs *for part-timers,* it is not done and never has been. *Wal-Mart is no different than other retailers.* They are not a factory or industry building cars, etc., who are forced to give huge incentives to employees because of union pressures....although many industries who offered health insurance, paid by them in the past, are now *forcing employees to pay much of the cost,* if not all.

It was reported recently that workers in the Detroit auto industry were making near $70.00 per hour including benefits. GM also has 435,000 former workers in retirement programs. Those are two huge clues why U.S. autos are high priced and why they keep losing business. In the same report, they said that the *amount of steel in a car cost less* than the benefit programs given to employees,

Besides the government programs like food stamps, etc., it is great that many Christian families and business firms are willing to furnish time, materials and money to fund government and private shelters, food pantries, the Salvation Army, Goodwill Industries, Red Cross, many churches, utilities helping with heat, etc., all who assist in providing help and assistance to those temporarily laid off or the 3% on

---

What are YOU going to do about it?

the very bottom of society who cannot get or hold a job for a variety of reasons as discussed above.

Many who work at Wal-Mart, Target, fast food places, small retailers, grocery stores, etc., are there because they want to be *and it fits into their needs and desires* or these are the only jobs they can qualify for. I'm talking about many *teens* looking for part time first or starter positions, millions of *young moms* with or without college education, looking for part time jobs to supplement the family income when their children reach school age, *seniors* needing a little extra cash or just something to do and looking for part time work and the handicapped who have some capabilities to work.

Part time workers are not looking for benefits like retirement programs, health plans, (many are covered by spouses or Medicare), etc. Very few, if any companies, give benefits to part time employees. It's never been done. Check out the employees next time you're in a fast food restaurant, retailer or big box company. It's easy to see the quality of some workers.

Liberals like to attack Wal-Mart and say that many of their workers are on Medicaid. The facts show that only 2% of Wal-Mart workers (after 2 years employment) are on Medicaid. (Well below the average for the general public). (I personally was a Chamber of Commerce Executive for many years and never had a retirement program).

New statistics regarding the *Minimum Wage* are quite revealing. Approximately 3.5 % of working people are getting the minimum wage or close to it, (only in some parts of the country). Further, *near 50%* of those *are teens* and/or going to school, 25% are part timers and 25% are in their first entry job. *Not* the severe problem created by liberals and the media. Many (3% to 5% of the public) are not capable of getting a higher paying position and some are not capable of *getting any kind of job.*

The Employment Policies Institute, a non-profit research organization, recently released the following unintended consequences. They found, that for every 10% increase in the minimum wage, unemployment among minorities rose 3.9% and 4.9% for Hispanics. Teen unemployment increased 6.6%. Among African-American teens it climbed 8.4%. And of course can you imagine what happened to the crime rate caused by teens?

What are YOU going to do about it?

A University of California-Irvine economist found that minimum wages have the largest negative effect on low-skilled employees, such as teens. James Sherk from the Heritage Foundation found, *"raising the minimum wage reduces many workers' job opportunities and working hours"*.

Sherk also found that relatively few workers earning the minimum wage "come from poor households". Interestingly, he found that, the average family *income of a minimum wage earner is nearly $50,000.* Now isn't that interesting? WOW! Never in the media!

The fit is perfect in these service businesses, both the workers and the business are very happy. It became very obvious *that these part time jobs* are what many are looking for when, in 2006, in the Chicago area, Wal-Mart was about to open a new store and had thousands apply for 2 or 3 hundreds jobs. It's what many want and many are only capable of that type of work *because of their situation in life* caused by many of the things we talked about above.

Another myth! Many liberals will say that, " Americans looking for a job, will take any job offered". It has been proven over and over that many agricultural jobs working in the fields of California and other States, hand picking fruits and vegetables in back breaking work, go under-manned (the starting pay is also near the $10.00 mark, not minimum). It has been reported this year (2007) some products have been unable to be harvested *because of a lack of workers* caused by tightening the borders. We frequently hear that many corporate farms are unable to find workers. When they go to an area where the workers hang out, waiting for jobs, they are laughed at by American workers who refuse to take these menial jobs.

The same thing happens in the hospitality business were some Americans, looking for jobs, refuse to take jobs requiring the scrubbing of pots, doing dishes, cleaning lavatories, making beds, bussing in restaurants, etc. *YES!!!* Some Americans (not all obviously) will not take many of these jobs!! They would rather stay on welfare or perhaps even a life of crime pushing drugs, robbing convenient stores or living with relatives or friends.

We continue to hear the *liberals say they will get rid of* President Bush's tax cuts, which brought our economy back to the best it has ever been. *They still don't get*

What are YOU going to do about it?

it*!* ***Every President that has cut taxes*** has seen the ***economy take enormous leaps***. Democrat ***President Kennedy started*** the longest economic expansion in history with tax cuts.

Then Carter raised taxes and saw a complete reversal. High inflation, high unemployment and double digit interest rates. Then came Reagan. Tax cuts brought 20 million new jobs, and interest and inflation dropped dramatically while unemployment dropped. Tax receipts doubled in the decade. Bush's tax cuts have done the same. The GDP has grown over 3% for 10 consecutive quarters and unemployment under 5%.

Christian Conservative Cal Thomas, in one of his weekly columns recently, wondered why we used to teach our young people the virtues of hard work, saving, personal responsibility and accountability for ones actions. Plus chastity before and fidelity and commitment in marriage, honesty, integrity and virtue? Thousands of business firms (near 20%) can't find trained help. Nursing, Sales, Plumbing, high tech.

Now, we teach entitlements, victim-hood, class envy and rights to other peoples money. It's called a tax, socialism, welfare, communism or all of the above!!!

CHAPTER VIII

MORE MEDIA BIAS:

We have given many solid and actual reasons how liberal media bias permeates our society. A recent informative program on TV showed interesting and unbelievable bias in two extremely radically liberal magazines. "Time" and "Newsweek". A study showed that over 90% of cover stories and cover pictures in the last few years or more, has shown the liberals in a very positive light with cover pictures of prominent Democrats/Liberals in full color and nice smiles or nicely framed and with positive stories to match. While nearly every picture of the President or other prominent Conservatives showed them in black and white, looking angry or cartoon like with negative stories questioning their claim to any positive position reported in the cover story. Cover after cover with no obvious attempt to hide their bias but yet these magazines publicly express that they are neutral.

A writer-producer for a hit liberal left wing TV show and a frequent liberal talking head on talk shows, reportedly said "there would never be any Republican show similar to it because the Hollywood Writers Guild of America, his union, is at minimum, *99% liberal"*. But strangely enough, all these radical entertainment elite continually insist they are not liberal! HA!

Movie star, Jane Fonda, used Black Panther, Communist, Marxist, Angela Davis as her mentor. Several of Fonda's college speeches here in the U.S. informed the students that Communism is the way to go and we should become a socialist society. Reportedly, Hillary Clinton had similar likes as she REPORTEDLY wrote her final college thesis on a famous Progressive Socialist.

And of course we are all familiar with other Hollywood radicals like Michael Moore! Most all of the Hollywood elite, directors, actors, actresses, etc., are all very radically liberal to the extreme. Interestingly, and probably the worst in Hollywood, Sean Penn, Danny Glover, Harry Belafonte and activist Cindy Sheehan, all have met individually with the hate monger President of Venezuela, Hugo Chavez. Chavez continually bashes the U.S., has declared that we are destroying the world, we have severe economic problems and we will implode shortly. (He is also a buddy of Castro).

In the same vein, a 2006 report showed that three prominent columnists of a major newspaper, over the last couple of years, have written 156 combined stories about the administration and the President. *Every one of the 156 were negative!* Not one positive! *"Say it enough times and it will become fact"!* If you read Bernard Goldberg's book, "Bias", and Ann Coulter's book "Slander", you'll get HUNDREDS OF SAMPLES OF the true picture of all the bias going on in the national media. (There are also several other very excellent books on the subject).

Some Examples: 89% of journalists voted for Clinton but only 16% of the total public. Only 4% of journalists consider themselves Republicans. In addition, a survey by the L.A. Times found that 82% of journalists *were pro-choice* but only 49% of the general public. 75% of the media were against prayer in schools, whereas 74% of the public thought it was OK. And we frequently find the liberal press and Democrats accusing the Republicans and the President of being out of touch with the public. *Who is out of touch?*

Editors of our local Gannett newspaper, reportedly said in a *weekly* editorial meeting, *that they seldom if*

What are YOU going to do about it?

ever hear or see the Presidents speeches or question and answer forums with the press or public, nor do they listen to C-Span or other news channels. Talk about being in the dark! WOW! They rely almost completely on the ultra *liberal AP* wire service for *canned national news*. Yet, they are quick to condemn the President's efforts and frequently editorialize against the U.S and Wisconsin CONSERVATIVES and their initiatives! Any bias there? I think we can also call that *"out of touch"!*

During the last few years, our local Gannett paper has refused to print about a dozen letters-to-the-editor or call-ins using material found in this book and by this writer. It became necessary to publish a book to get the real story out to the public. The media refuses to do it and will give dozens of reasons why they can't!

PERHAPS THE MOST GREVIOUS LIBERAL MEDIA SLANDER HAS TO DO WITH THE IRAQ WAR. Example: Reports indicated that returning military were killing massive number of citizens. Wrong!! Actually lower rate than average population. Any apologys..no! Military deaths in peacetime 1980 same as during 2006 at the height of the insurgency.

GUILTY BEFORE INDICTMENT!

*T*he liberals and the press continually, for many weeks in '06, insinuated/speculated and led the public to believe, that Presidential Assistant Rove and Senate majority leader Frist were in deep trouble and indictments were shortly coming. All speculation! *Guilty in the eyes of the press* and liberals before even being indicted, *let alone put to trial!* Nothing *ever became of any supposed charges.* They also speculated that the administration and the President would be destroyed by this scandal. More ridiculous insinuations! Anything to win an election!!!

The worst and truly defaming were the Democratic leaders, Pelosi, Kennedy, Dean, Reid, et al, SCREAMING FROM THE ROOF TOPS that the administration was corrupt, dishonest, liars, etc. (Of course, *conveniently* not mentioning all the prior scandals of the Democrats nor reporting that *55 out of the last 70 investigations in Congress* were against Democrats -- many for jail time). *Has the media* told you that? More double standard reporting by the nations media! Do we see a *pattern* here?

What are YOU going to do about it?

Unfortunately, some of the most vulnerable public listens to this garbage and believes it! (And we wonder why the Presidents ratings go down--*strictly brainwashing* by the media and liberal democrats). That's all the public hears on all national TV and press including Gannett and USA Today and on the AP wires to all media.

Even locally we hear news commentators, nearly every night, leading their newscast with....."the Iraq death toll reached __ today, one of the worst weeks or months in the war with ___deaths in Baghdad and _____". Have we heard that type reporting in any other war or conflict in the past? NO! Anything to *discredit the President!* I guess it's easier this time because of the miniscule number of deaths, not like the hundreds or even thousands getting killed daily *like in other wars and conflicts.* Average only two per day by enemy action in Iraq! **WE ACTUALLY HAD MORE MILITARY DEATHS IN PEACETIME (1980) THAN WE HAVE HAD DURING THE HEIGHT OF THE INSURGENCY IN IRAQ (2006).** Just proves how miniscule the number of deaths are in Iraq.

Strange, but as usual, the liberal democrats and media conveniently forget the *Democrat corruption* of the past. Clinton and Hillary's problems in Arkansas that saw many of their business partners *convicted,* (Hillary was very close to being indicted), or how about the many election problems in Chicago over the years and elsewhere with the local Democratic machine stealing votes, dead people voting, or how soon they forget the seldom mentioned *draft dodger Clinton* decided on a plea agreement (while President) and offered to pay one of his sexual partners $90,000 and paid a $25,000 fine for obstruction of justice and was disbarred as a lawyer. (That's not even mentioning his moral problems). (As President)!!!

Or how about the liberal Florida Congressman who is being investigated for bribery and the FBI finding $90,000 in his freezer at home and then being re-elected by his predominately African-American constituents. There was no sign of any action by Democrats to remove him from office. In fact he got a *standing ovation* from his black Congressional caucus and *no media or Congressional condemnation* that *usually* accompanies even suggested Conservative wrong-doings even before indictments, before trials!!!

Then there's Sandy Berger, of the *Clinton* Administration, *who hid secret papers* in his socks

---

What are YOU going to do about it?

and then destroyed them—(reportedly about the 9-11 attack), just before the 9-11 hearings started. He *plead guilty and paid a $50,000 fine.* No democrat outrage. (He has refused to take a lie detector test that he agreed to take).

There are many others to numerous to mention. Double standards—you bet! *More than outrages!!* But of course, throw Libby *in jail* for a *FEW LIES!!* HE'S A CONSERVATIVE!!!

ACTUAL – WORD FOR WORD – IN COURT!!!

Attorney: She had three children, right??
Witness: Yes!!
Attorney: How many were boys??
Witness: None!!
Attorney: Were there any girls???

           UGH!!!

RECOMMENDED READINGS:

Reading the following will more than back-up my studies within this book.

Strangely, I did not read any of these before writing my book. Most all the material in my book was assembled prior to any of these books being published. JCH

"182 DAYS IN IRAQ" by Phil Kiver

"THE CONNECTION" by Stephen F. Hayes

"THE ENEMY WITHIN" by Michael Savage

"SLANDER" by Ann Coulter

"INVESTORS BUSINESS DAILY"
A daily newspaper similar to the Wall Street Journal

"THE PROFESSORS - THE 101 MOST DANGEROUS ACADEMICS IN AMERICA"
By David Horowitz

"INDOCTRINATION U."----By David Horowitz

"BIAS"—By Bernard Goldberg

What are YOU going to do about it?

CPSIA information can be obtained
at www.ICGtesting.com
Printed in the USA
BVHW011359270420
578617BV00005B/140